'It has helped me in so many different ways to understand myself and also be more kind to myself. I keep referring back to it when I have difficult moments and it always helps me, even if it's in a small way.'

'This book was one of the few things that I found comfort in while experiencing a depressive episode recently.'

'I found this such an eloquent but honest read that was at no point even remotely condescending. From the get go it was as though I was reading about myself. I owe the author a thank you.'

'I wish someone would have given me this book when I was 15. If you're struggling with mental health problems, this book is for you.'

'As a parent of a child with mental health problems, this is an amazing resource.'

'This book makes me feel less alone, and I wish 13 year old me could've read it. I would like everyone to read it whether mentally ill or not.'

'I bought three copies of this book, because I knew I had to give it to my friends and I wouldn't be able to let go of my copy. It is brilliant - emotional and practical, talking about mental illness with complete understanding of its grip, and also the necessity of dealing with it, in big and small ways.'

'This book is essential reading for anyone who has a mental illness and anyone who doesn't. I wish that it had existed when I was younge   ou for
writing such

'Incredible book, I felt as though someone peeked into my head and wrote it all down.'

'This book helped more than anything else I tried. Whether you're suffering or you know somebody who is, this book is utterly invaluable.'

'A fantastic book. It's funny, it's concise, and it holds no illusions about what it means to live with mental illness. I read it as an adult, but I wish someone had given it to me as a child.'

'I've never related to any writing on mental health the way I did to this.'

'I've spent years searching for a manual for survival like this. I cannot express how grateful I am to Emily for her honesty and wisdom of lived experience.'

'Warm, down to earth, funny, practical - Emily writes as the wise, seen-some-things friend that we all need when dealing with mental illness.'

'Just a fantastic book. There were so many moments and feelings that I recognised instantly and it's written in such an honest and unflinchingly raw way that it perfectly captures what it's like living with mental illness.'

'I am sure that it will be a book I return to again and again, as a tonic and as a manual.'

'Such a warm, funny, unflinching book; startlingly pragmatic and written with so much kindness, I loved it.'

'I recommend this especially to younger people but honestly, to everybody. I know I'll be revisiting it time and time again - it's full of bookmarks that will ensure it!'

A
BEGINNER'S GUIDE
TO LOSING
YOUR MIND

EMILY REYNOLDS

yellow
kite

First published in Great Britain in 2017 by Yellow Kite
An imprint of Hodder & Stoughton
An Hachette UK company

This paperback edition published in 2018

1

A CIP catalogue record for this title is available from the British Library

B format ISBN 9781473635630
eBook ISBN 9781473635647

Typeset in New Baskerville ITC by
Palimpsest Book Production Limited, Falkirk, Stirlingshire

Printed and bound in Great Britain by Clays Ltd, St Ives plc

Hodder & Stoughton policy is to use papers that are natural, renewable
and recyclable products and made from wood grown in sustainable
forests. The logging and manufacturing processes are expected to
conform to the environmental regulations of the country of origin.

CONTENTS

Introduction   1

1. Diagnosis   9

2. Self-Care   30

3. Dating   62

4. Education   88

5. Self-Harm and Suicide   121

6. Family and Friends   148

7. The Internet   176

8. Recovery and Relapse   191

Resources   213

Acknowledgements   219

Index   223

INTRODUCTION

Being diagnosed with bipolar was the happiest moment of my life. Forget falling in love, graduation, the birth of my nephew . . . All that schmaltzy, saccharine stuff pales in comparison to hearing the words: 'You have bipolar 1 disorder.' Meeting the love of your life? Not a big deal, really. Throwing your mortar board in the air as the symbolic climax of three years of intellectual challenge and growth? Whatever. Sitting in a dingy, grey office as a psychiatrist says, 'Yes, you *do* have a chronic mental illness?' Now *that's* what I'm talking about.

Of course, I'm being flippant, but it's really not that much of an exaggeration. My road to diagnosis was long and hard, punctuated with hours of numb staring in indistinguishable waiting rooms. It took ten years from the first signs of mental illness – ten years of appointments with psychiatrists and GPs and badly trained counsellors; ten years of misdiagnosis and medication that made me sick or fat or even more ill. I can reel off the names of the pills I've taken (SSRIs and MAOIs and tricyclic antidepressants and atypical antipsychotics . . .) like a child drably reciting times tables by rote; and the mis-diagnoses too – major depression, borderline personality disorder and a good smattering of 'You'll probably feel better in a few weeks'. I've accepted, rejected, then finally accepted again my status as 'someone with mental health problems'. It's been a journey in the sense that it has been a gruelling physical challenge, and also in the *X-Factor*, sob-story sense. So, while it might just be the beauty of narrative hindsight, the day I was diagnosed felt like a culmination of all of these elements.

* * *

I first experienced mental health problems when I was around thirteen or fourteen years old. They seemed to come on unprompted, and at first I couldn't really put my finger on what was wrong or how I was even feeling. Groggy, a lot of the time, and with a lack of concentration that I put down to regular disinterest in school and my peers. Then I started to get dizzy – so much so that I felt as if I was floating outside my own body, unable to cling on to any of my sensory abilities whatsoever. (I later learned that this is what's referred to clinically as dissociation – a detachment from your physical and emotional surroundings.) I would gaze out of the window on the bus home, watching houses and shops fly past, but unable to connect the images to anything I could even remotely identify as my 'self'.

I was also viciously sad; I would sleep almost constantly, had absolutely no interest in anything, with the only thing that would alleviate the stagnant numbness being an addiction to self-harm that I indulged in at home and in the school toilets at lunchtime. I didn't think I could possibly be ill, though. I didn't even entertain the idea.

The problem lay partly in the fact that many of the symptoms of depression, or bipolar, are similar to traits that are also considered to be ubiquitous in teenagers. The difference was the severity and duration, but that's hard to communicate when you're fourteen, terminally shy and haven't got the language to express what you're feeling. Skim reading the Wikipedia article for Sartre and viewing my malaise as some kind of profound existential statement about the world didn't help either. It was as though the terrible feelings of suffocation were a logical, intellectual choice – a personality trait or a philosophy I'd chosen, rather than an illness that had so much power over me.

It wasn't. I was depressed.

I was finally diagnosed, ten years later, in the midst of my worst ever depressive episode. I had dealt badly with a break-up, and days spent crying over my ex had turned into weeks of not getting out of bed and, eventually, a few months of almost complete stasis. I barely ate, I saw nobody, I did nothing but sleep and cry. I cried so much that I became physically unable to muster a solitary tear, and it took nearly a year of stable, medicated living before I was able to cry again. (Incidentally, I ended up finally losing it over a dog-food advert. It wasn't quite the significant cinematic experience I was hoping for, but y'know . . . I'll take what I can get.)

Eventually, I was no longer even slightly bothered about my break-up, and I realised that all the sobbing and sleeping and the inability to eat – not knowing whether today would be the day when I finally conjured up enough courage to throw myself under a bus – were because I was actually deeply ill. It kind of sucked, actually, because at least the break-up had been something to focus on. Where was I without it?

You might have thought that understanding that I was ill would have made it all a lot easier. I was used to the rigma-role of the whole thing, after all: feeling shitty for a while, going to the doctor and getting medication, settling down after some nausea and teeth-grinding and then feeling OK again. But this time it was somehow harder; something inside me was proving such a profound source of resistance that I was absolutely incapable of doing anything.

I really don't know what did it, but one day that resistance snapped and I pressingly felt that it was imperative for me to go back to the doctor as soon as I possibly could. So I did. I went to my local GP surgery and saw a doctor I'd never seen before. I was apprehensive, but only as much as anyone normally is when they go to the doctor. But when I told her I was suicidal, she dismissed it immediately. 'Why are you sad?' she asked, failing even to glance at my extensive medical notes. I explained that there was no reason – I was just ill. But she kept pressing: there *must* be a reason. My already pretty weak resolve was dissolving with every question when, halfway through the consultation, after I told her to actually look at the notes that would corroborate what I was saying, she asked me whether I was interested in giving up smoking. Eventually, she sent me away, telling me that if I was still suicidal in two weeks I should go back and see her again. It didn't seem to cross her mind that if I was no longer suicidal in two weeks, it might be because I was dead.

My local mental health trust was no more helpful; I needed to be referred or sectioned, and I had neither such qualifica-tion. At the hospital I was handed a leaflet for Alcoholics Anonymous and a tissue, so I suppose they beat the GP if only in terms of paper consumption.

I was defeated. Crushed and small and defeated. I was filled with a sick, desperate urgency that clawed at everything I did, and that was seemingly incommunicable. I felt nauseous with despair, and had a restless, unfulfilled desire to do something, although what I wasn't sure. It had become a ceaseless effort to move from bed to bathroom; now, I had somehow dragged myself to hospital only to be told I wasn't quite ill enough.

Luckily, and contrary to the experiences of the vast majority of psychiatric patients, I managed to get an appointment to see a private psychiatrist, who took the time to listen to me and properly evaluate my situation.*

I think I already knew on some level that I had bipolar, and it was probably quite obvious to anyone who had spent more than five minutes with me when manic. One of my friends told me that the first time we met, I'd spewed a nonsensical torrent of word soup at him non-stop for twenty minutes, before announcing that I was off to meet up with an ex-boyfriend. I'd also, at various times, got myself into thousands of pounds' worth of debt, relocated across the country – twice – and signed up for and started three degree courses, only one of which I managed to finish.

My life up until this point had mainly been defined by my periods of depression, though, mainly because my teenage years of Morrissey fandom and self-harm had come at such a persona-defining time I'd never thought of my mania

* I'm a huge fan of the NHS, but resources are so stretched that it's just impossible to experience the same level of care as you do privately. Funding for mental health care has fallen year on year since the last election, so my decision to go private was a (very privileged) choice I made for personal, rather than political, reasons.

as being a problem. I think I saw it more as just 'the way I am'. A more exaggerated version, maybe, but still a far more accurate and desirable one than the laconic, unwashed slob I became when depressed. My mania had never seemed problematic purely because it was so much fun – the nights out, the sparkling conversations I thought I was having, the way I felt absolutely, unimpeachably sexually magnetic.

It was only once I moved to London and lived alone that I realised how massively mania impacted my life; I was emotionally and physically reckless in a way that alarmed and eventually alienated my close friends. I was bad with money but had no student loan or parental handouts to fall back on. I had a full-time job as well as a packed social schedule that involved endless parties and up to six dates per weekend. I needed less sleep than usual, but it was still profoundly exhausting. I started to conceptualise my mental health differently: maybe it wasn't the dark, motionless days of depression that really defined my state of mind, but the insatiable need for stimulation that came with mania as well.

* * *

Throughout my journey from undiagnosed teenager to fully paid-up member of the Certifiably Insane Club, my mental health irrevocably affected almost every area of my life. My education, career, family life, sex life, self-image – every single way in which a person can relate to themselves and the world – were all scuppered by it. And I've learned the hard way how not to date when you're ill, how to communicate your illness (or not) to colleagues, how best to navigate the rocky road of medication and therapy. I wish I'd had someone to tell me all of this, though, wish I hadn't messed up so many friendships and relationships and jobs with my inability to accept that my bipolar puts obstacles in my path.

So: here is this book. There wasn't anything like it when I was going through all of these things, and I wish there had been, so I've written it. Don't get me wrong, I've read plenty of self-help books too. But when you can't even take a shower, a book that tells you how to 'focus your mind on success' or suggests that you 'ask the universe for the things you want' kind of falls short. All I want to do is ask the universe: 'Make me not ill, pal. I just wanna be able to wash my hair like everyone else.'

There are plenty of books about mental health, but they never really resonated with me or my experiences. There are narcissistic misery memoirs that romanticise the fuck out of mental illness and offer wild ideas of 'redemption through love' or some other nonsense; and there are clinical books that offer no emotional insight into illness. There was never anything that bridged the gap between 'I identify with this person's experience, and it helps me feel less alone' and 'this is genuinely useful advice that I can apply to my own life'. So here we are.

I hope that this book will help anyone who has had similar experiences, or maybe totally different ones, to understand their mental health problems a little better, or at least to gather some ideas on how to effectively manage them. I hope they can avoid some of my horrible mistakes, or at the very least feel comforted that they're not the only ones who blurt out their diagnosis on a date or live like a trash-raiding raccoon when they're depressed.

And for those who aren't ill, I hope this will provide a small insight into what it's like to live with a chronic mental health problem, shatter a few myths and offer a rough framework through which others who might be affected too can be supported.

This book will be sad, and sometimes it will be brutal. We'll be looking at self-harm, suicide, drug abuse and more, and much of this will make for difficult reading, especially if you have had experience of it. All of the chapter titles are clearly marked, so please do give yourself a break if you think the subject matter might negatively affect you. It'll also be gross, because the reality of mental illness often is, but it might make you laugh as well. There are guides and lists throughout, so there's a strong practical element, and while I'm loath to call it self-help, because self-help books can so often be trite and useless, my hope is that it will make you feel comforted, empowered or even just slightly less alone.

CHAPTER 1

DIAGNOSIS

It was an unseasonably brisk October evening when I strode out of my psychiatrist's office with a piece of paper that said I definitely had something wrong with me. For the first time in months I felt something that vaguely resembled hope, and while I wouldn't go so far as to say I felt positive, I felt buoyed up by this unexpected life jacket, surprised at how snugly it fit. As he had sombrely delivered his diagnosis I thought to myself 'Don't look too happy, Emily. He'll think you're making it all up'.

I've already said it was the happiest moment of my life, and I mean it. Although I was obviously still deeply depressed, the horrible buzzing noise in my head that told me things would never get better briefly ceased. I felt calm, steady and determined. Ready to get better.

Unfortunately, the reason I was so serene was because my understanding of what it meant to 'get better' was wildly off the mark. I saw knowing what was wrong with me as the very first step on the journey to sanity – the end of a tangled ball of string that would eventually lead me to my final facedown with the Minotaur that was my mental illness. I thought that being armed with self-knowledge (and a hefty dose of antipsychotics) was the magical key to a previously unknown realm in which breakthrough and profundity were the order of the day.

This is not how it works.

What I had failed to take into consideration was my relationship with myself, my self-image. The way I conceptualised myself as a girlfriend or a daughter or just as a person was all tightly bound up with mental illness, correct label be damned. It didn't matter if I was bipolar or depressed or had borderline personality disorder – I might as well have flipped through the DSM* and randomly jabbed my finger at a set of diagnostic criteria. What really mattered, and what I didn't understand that day, was how much of my personality was dependent on 'mental illness' as a vague, nebulous concept, rather than as a strict scientific definition.

And aside from this, diagnosis can often be completely arbitrary. Studies have shown that despite standardised diagnostic criteria being widely used in the Western world, identical sets of symptoms can be identified as totally different conditions by different doctors. And cultural variations come into play too: behaviours that are considered to be social norms in some cultures can be pathologised in others. So, it turns out, diagnosis is not the most important element of the mental health journey.

The thing about mental illness – in whatever guise, under

---

* The DSM – or Diagnostic and Statistical Manual of Mental Disorders, to give it its full name – is the handbook used by doctors and psychiatrists to diagnose particular symptoms and conditions. It's pretty ubiquitous – you won't find a psychiatrist without one – but has also been the subject of controversy with regards to overdiagnosis, validity, and the medicalisation of human experience. *Saving Normal* by Allen Frances covers this far better than me!

whatever name – is that it plagues you with profound self-doubt. 'Am I really depressed?' you ask yourself. 'Or am I just lazy?' 'Is my inability to hold on to money because I have manic episodes, or am I just an irresponsible person?' 'Is my near constant craving for chemical stimulation a coping mechanism I've developed to deal with my problems, or do I just really, really like drugs?' It's an annoying voice in your ear, like a director's commentary endlessly droning over all the best bits of the film.

Obviously some parts of your life *are* affected by mental illness. Of course you'll be anti-social when you're depressed, dangerously cavalier when you're manic, avoidant and nervous when you're anxious. But this pathological overanalysing doesn't stop at the bad parts, the wobbly teeth of your personality that you can't help but push at – it envelops everything. So the good parts are hit by it too, in a different way, as you ask yourself whether your mental illness is actually responsible for the few traits you like in yourself. Am I truly an empathetic person? Do I really care about other people, or am I just experiencing the pathetic recognition of a fellow loser? Am I outgoing and fun, or am I hopped up on mania, too brash and loud to realise how obnoxious I really am?

Doctors talk about 'overidentification', where, as I've said, you ascribe every aspect of your character to your illness. It can be hard not to do this, especially if you've been ill since you were a teenager. Adolescence is a time where you begin to grope blindly for the light switch of your own character. And if the one thing that keeps you company throughout those years is mental illness, it's hard not to feel like it's everything you are. Which parts are me? Which parts are bipolar?

Diagnosis both helps and hinders this process. It helps in that it validates those doubts: yes, you are depressed, yes, your anxiety is real. But it doesn't quieten the other voice, the part that asks you who you'd be without your mental illness. It doesn't simplify the confused mess of mixed-up feelings. It doesn't help you untangle the origin of each one. And it doesn't tell you where each of them should sit inside of you.

* * *

I started seeing a therapist just after I'd dropped out of my first degree. He was snooty and cold and unapproachable (thus making him pretty useless as a therapist). He attributed everything I said – every fucking thing – to 'self-destruction', like it was enjoyable for me to have been psychotic, to feel so desperately sad; like I had absolutely no control over my behaviour whatsoever.

I remember sitting in one of our first few sessions, midway through some rant or other (and knowing me at nineteen, probably quoting a slightly misremembered Wikipedia-d Camus passage or something), when he interrupted me and asked, 'Don't you want to get better?' And honestly? The answer was no.

Like I say, it wasn't that I *enjoyed* being ill – clearly, obviously, I did not. I'd just had a psychotic episode in which, for two days, I had legitimately thought I was dead. I don't remember much about it, but I do know that I lay in a single bed in my tiny university room, not eating or drinking or using the bathroom, somehow convinced that I was invisible, a ghost. An actual, real-life ghost. Like Casper, if he'd spent the past year on the set of *Animal House*. It sounds really stupid; I still think about it and wonder how it happened, desperately searching for memories about it, for reasoning: what was I *thinking*? Also, what was I literally thinking?

I'm not sure about causality, but the episode did correlate with a crash – the end of my first year at university. I'd spent both terms drinking heavily and sleeping erratically, some days for four hours, some for sixteen. My initial spurt of enthusiasm and productivity slowly trickled away and, by Christmas, I wasn't going to lectures. As the term wore on I became less and less social. Gone were the days where I'd go out drinking and dancing four times a week. By this point, I wasn't leaving my room unless it was absolutely vital. I started visiting the communal kitchen at night to ensure that I didn't bump into any of my housemates (more on whom later). Eventually, I started ordering food online and having it delivered directly to my door, only buying things that didn't require cooking, so that I never, ever had to leave my room. For the two weeks before my psychotic episode began, I consumed nothing but four packets of Skips a day, which I had ordered in multipacks (if you were wondering: no, I still can't bear the taste of them), washing it all down with three 500ml cans of energy drink a day, which probably didn't help my already fractious state of mind.

I'd broken up with my boyfriend a few weeks previously, a life event that *always* acts as a catalyst for breakdown for me. It's not even that I particularly loved him – I emphatically didn't. It was just a change in routine, a jolt. I think he could tell there was something going on, his nervous disposition betraying abject terror at my state of mind. (To add further absurdity to the situation, he'd split up with me while dressed as a cow.)

After the break-up I started obsessively scanning his

Facebook and Twitter accounts, trying to work out which club or pub he'd be going to that night. I'd then turn up, alone, and start talking to both him and strangers, expelling reams of garbled nonsense at top speed. And when I say nonsense I don't mean standard drunk-student fare; I mean actual gibberish, non-sequiturs, sentences that tumbled out side by side at random, bearing no relation to one another, words springing from my mouth in an order I couldn't predict. Most of these nights ended with me hysterical, being escorted back to my room by a bemused stranger or unsympathetic acquaintance. I often wonder what those people thought was happening; whether, as drunk freshers, they understood that in front of them was a person unravelling, or whether they were cruel behind my back and wrote it off as my being a 'crazy bitch'. I suspect the latter, because we were all eighteen and everyone is dumb at that age. There's more advice for friends and family later on in the book, if you want to avoid being These People.

Years before this, years before I ever touched alcohol or lived alone, and way before I was allowed to just sleep whenever I wanted, I was miserable. I self-harmed from the age of thirteen and was suicidal from fifteen, conducting long Socratic dialogues with myself weighing up the relative costs and benefits of life versus death.

I was never well liked at school. I suspect that to begin with I gave off the desperate air of someone keen to be accepted, before morphing into a difficult, contrary girl who cared little about being liked and for whom aggravating people, provoking them on purpose, became a full-time hobby. Despite having light, downy blonde hair I was mocked for having hairy legs, so I deliberately and permanently stopped shaving them.

Because I had listed myself as bisexual on my Myspace profile, the word 'dyke' was hissed at me in corridors and classrooms, to which I responded by writing more frequently and aggressively in notes and bulletins and blogs about my attraction to women.

But this label of 'outsider' was something that I thrived on, revelled in, and my poor mental health was an important part of that. I was proud of it, in a way. And it was probably the main reason I was disliked, actually, rather than any of the arbitrary things that I was picked on for. I was unsettled, and therefore unsettling.

As many teenagers do, I also found solace in things that reflected how I felt. I passionately loved the music of Morrissey and the Smiths (so much so that I'm pretty sure some of my peers probably still think of me as 'that weird Morrissey girl'), and I'd read and learned by rote most of Sylvia Plath's poems. All very clichéd, I know this now, but these songs and poems were the centre of my world and I defined myself by them. The threads that ran through all of these passions were, obviously, misery and melancholia. It was comforting, but was it enjoyable? No. So why, then, five years later, was I telling a therapist that I didn't want to get better? It was exactly *because* of all this.

I felt like my identity was so wrapped up in my unhappiness that I wouldn't be anything without it. If I was happy, or at the very least not-unhappy, there'd be nothing to me. I'd be one of those weird undressed mannequins with no head. Ground zero, *tabula rasa*. And I would have to fill all of that up with other stuff – stuff that made me happy, I guessed, but what would that involve? Everyone's suggestions seemed arbitrary and useless. I got a job in a supermarket at my mum's behest and it did make me more sociable and less insular, but stacking shelves does not a contented person make. What else was there? Someone suggested Open University, but my pride was still too wounded from having had to drop out of my previous course to do that. Join a book club? Learn to knit? Write more? Get a boyfriend? I did all of these things, and none of them helped. They were just that: things. Without my mental illness I felt rudderless, unmoored, lost.

My sadness, in particular, was something I clung onto like a security blanket; I knew it, felt safe with it, understood its subtleties and nuances in a way I never quite did with happiness. Have you ever nervously entered a room full of people you don't really know and felt so awkward that you suddenly, self-consciously, don't know what to do with your arms? That's how happiness felt to me. I couldn't quite grasp it; I didn't know how to support it or live beside it. It felt like an effort – an endless Sisyphean feat that required faculties I didn't think I would ever possess. Do you learn to be happy? Does it just happen to you? I had no idea. Unhappiness was a known quantity. It was easier.

All of this increased tenfold when I finally received my diagnosis. It was confirmation of every thought I'd ever had about 'just being a naturally unhappy person', every doubt I'd ever harboured about my ability to be happy. I was right. It was all true. I wasn't exaggerating. I wasn't making it up. There was *something wrong with me*: a disease not only of my brain, but of my very essence.

I think some of it was performative too. How else to deal with being called crazy all the time other than by playing up to it? It was like my resolute refusal to shave as a teenager.

I'd been criticised for something, so how better to react than by intensifying that behaviour? By acting 'mad', or at least by refusing to hide this madness from other people, it felt like I was proving it to them. It seems childish, and it probably was, but mad people are so rarely believed, so often dismissed, that it seemed vital to my continued existence. If people didn't know what I was, I wouldn't know how to act at all, their inattention making me almost completely invisible. To say my behaviour was an extended 'cry for help' would probably be disingenuous; it was just a cry to be heard – to say, 'I am here and I am in pain'. I needed it to be validated.

Diagnosis was also a huge relief because it allowed me to completely discard any sense of personal responsibility. On some level I always knew I was ill, and sometimes to my shame I used it as an excuse, but I tried to keep this to a minimum. I wanted to be sure I wasn't selling myself short or, more importantly, hurting anybody else. But as soon as I started thinking about myself as 'a bipolar person' rather than just 'Emily' things started to go a little downhill for me.

As you will find out later in the book, the first thing to go when I'm depressed is my personal hygiene and my grip on how tidy my home is. I could see it happening, and often felt powerless as an army of unwashed plates and dirty T-shirts marched slowly and silently towards my prone, actionless body, but I always had a deep desire to stop it in its tracks. As soon as I was diagnosed, though, I started seeing everything through the lens of my mental illness, even when I wasn't feeling particularly bad. Two lazy days would turn into two lazy weeks, as laundry piled up and dishes sat stagnant in the sink – but by playing the Mental Card I was able to lie to myself, justify putting it off. 'This is just what happens when I get depressed,' I calmly told myself. 'I can't *help* it . . . When I'm depressed I just *can't* clean, so . . .' I wasn't depressed, though; I just couldn't be arsed and, finally, I had an excuse.

It's the same with mania. A few years ago, newly single and somewhat heartbroken, I found myself gripped by the intense existential terror of being alone. I was going on five dates a week, with one guy I was seeing regularly. He was older than me, could clearly tell I was ill and had started doing everything he could to try and make me feel better or look after me. I think we both realised fairly early on that it wasn't going to be true love, but he would come round and watch films with me, or we'd go to the pub and enthusiastically debate Morrissey B-sides. He was lovely, in short.

But then another relentless wave of mania smashed down on me and swept all his good work away. I proceeded to invite him out to a bar, completely ignore him when he turned up and then kissed someone else in front of him without saying a single word to him all night. The next morning I woke up hung over, coming down and filled with a level of interminable dread that I've never felt before or since. I pushed it to the back of my mind on a lazy Susan spinning endlessly with distractions: Facebook, Twitter, Facebook, chat with a friend on the phone, Twitter, a line of coke. I didn't shower for four days (a shower meant I would be alone with my thoughts, which meant my mind would inevitably wander to the fact that I was a shitty, selfish person). I couldn't bear to inhabit my own body.

Even now I feel a sense of deep, crushing shame when I think about it. It makes me feel breathless with horror, even though in the grand scheme of things it isn't that bad. I didn't steal the guy's credit card or run over someone's pet rabbit. But the incident did act as a kind of mirror to myself for the sort of person I have the potential to be if I were to lose control of my alcohol intake or drug use. And what better way of dealing with that than blaming it on mental illness?

Overidentifying with my diagnosis led me to justify my bad life choices with an abandon I had never previously afforded myself. It let me act in a totally self-serving way – you know, those things you always *want* to do but know you can't or shouldn't. It's the perfect excuse for not being bigger or better, for not taking the positive steps needed to become the person that you really want to be. And in a way it's childlike, safe and warm, curled up in an amniotic sac of guiltlessness. Said something stupid at work? Bipolar. Slept with someone you probably shouldn't have? Bipolar. Flaked out on your friends yet again because you can't be bothered to leave the house? It's not because I'm unreliable – um, *actually*, I have bipolar?

And it can also allow you to fail. Sometimes you fuck up at work or say the wrong thing to your partner during an argument. That's normal. But using your diagnosis can be a shortcut here, a way to not analyse why you've done or said something stupid or thoughtless. Of course, mental illness *does* fuck up your career and your love life sometimes, and sometimes it *can* be the reason you do these things, but often it just isn't relevant at all. By endlessly blaming your actions on it, though, you fail to have any accountability.

It's passive, sure, but being fucked-up can be a choice in itself, and it's quite often the easier one. Thinking that everything you do, good or bad, can be totally explained by your mental illness? That helps. Nobody expects anything of you; you don't expect anything of yourself. It stops the dreaded footsteps of adulthood and responsibility from encroaching on your selfish, self-indulgent plans. It is the ultimate get-out clause.

When I didn't want to think about how much I had hurt someone who cared about me, telling myself it was because I was bipolar was the only way I would deal with it. I definitely wouldn't have done it if I wasn't manic, but mania often exaggerates facets of yourself that already exist. Am I a slut or a sociopath or any of the other names that could have been justifiably thrown at me that night? Probably not. But I am sometimes selfish and irresponsible, and often capricious. I was a caricature of myself, one of those portraits you get on holiday where your head is huge and you have googly eyes and a giant mouth. But cartoon or not, it was still me.

Living my life with my diagnosis tattooed on my brain, reciting it like a rosary every time I made a false move, is the single biggest mistake I've made. It meant I never thought about my actions, it removed my agency, it disempowered me. It made me a passive victim of my poor mental health. It should have done the opposite. I should have continued to feel as positive and enthusiastic as I did the day I first received it. But ultimately, it allowed me to absolve myself of all responsibility. Being happy isn't just a choice, of course; I have a medical illness that no amount of positive thinking or introspection can get rid of.

Diagnosis isn't some kind of magical solve-all requiring no effort on your behalf. But it *was* a stepping stone for me to working all of my shit out, and I was right in thinking it was the first step. It is a landmark point on any mental health journey, and can open lots of different doors for you. We'll be exploring the ways in which it can be a brilliant, life-changing thing a bit later. But first: how to get diagnosed in the first place.

How to Get Successfully Diagnosed

As you can see, my journey to diagnosis was long and complicated and mainly characterised by introspection. But what about the actual, tangible reality – the doctor's visits, the endless script you have to learn by rote to be heard? How do you actually *get diagnosed*?

This is how it went for me, chronologically speaking:

- Age fourteen, fifteen, sixteen and seventeen: repeat visits to GP in an attempt to get diagnosed with depression. Am ignored and told I am 'just a teenager'.
- Age eighteen: full-on psychotic episode. Finally given medication and therapy for depression. Psychosis totally ignored by doctor. Aforementioned therapist claims I'm 'probably just a bit stressed'.
- Age nineteen: given free therapy on NHS. It helps with my anxiety, but it only lasts for six sessions and after a while I'm back to square one.
- Age nineteen, twenty, twenty-one: more visits to GP in attempt to get medication that does something other than make me feel worse. Am prescribed new drugs. They don't work. Go back to doctor. Get new drugs or higher doses. Repeat ad infinitum. Eventually stop taking medication.
- Age twenty-three: second psychotic episode. Auditory and visual hallucinations. See a psychiatrist who *actually asks what my symptoms are*. Finally get diagnosis, medication and therapy that fit.

So what's the pattern here? What can you learn from nearly ten years of misdiagnosis, thoughtlessly prescribed medication and dismissed symptoms? Sadly, it's that getting diagnosed, even being believed, can be really fucking hard.

Don't get me wrong, I've had some great experiences with deeply empathetic GPs, and with some who brusquely and refreshingly treat my bipolar in the same way they would a stomach ulcer: it's a medical fact, it's affecting your life, these are the steps we're taking to fix it. But there have been several who have been truly awful, who clearly don't care too much about mental illness or thought I was exaggerating or a hypochondriac. And while after ten years of this, I now have the language to argue my point with them, when I first started going? No way.

So what do you do when you think you're ill and you have to convince your doctor you need help? What do you say if they tell you to 'come back in two weeks' or ask you if you've considered taking up running? Here's a guide.

Book, and go to, the appointment

This may seem like a really, really obvious point – 'to get a doctor's appointment, just book an appointment!' – but it can be the hardest part. Finding the courage to actually call your GP surgery and make an appointment is *terrifying*. But a few things to remember.

- One: the receptionist does not need to know what the appointment is about. They may ask, but don't feel you have to tell them if it makes you uncomfortable.
- Two: you can book a double appointment. They're only about fifteen minutes long, which is no time at all, but

the extra five or ten minutes this will afford you may make a big difference in terms of the depth of discussion you have with your doctor and how comfortable you feel.

- Three: remember there is *absolutely no shame in asking for help if you need it*. You have not failed. You are not weak. You are *not making it up*. What you're doing is brave and important and responsible; you're looking after yourself, loving yourself and respecting yourself.

And yes, going to the appointment is also hard. You will probably feel nervous and have a million doubts: 'What if they think I'm making it up?' 'What if I *am* making it up?' 'Am I a fraud?' 'What if I make a fool of myself?' 'What if they won't help me?' These questions and more will probably race *ad nauseam* around your head.

Plan in advance (see below). Take a deep breath. Ask a friend to hold your hand or distract you, if needed. If you're really nervous, you can take your friend to the appointment with you too, and they can support what you're saying if you're finding it hard.

Be prepared

Preparation is the key here. Be equipped to answer certain questions, and have those answers ready ('How long have you been feeling like this?' 'Do you have any desire to harm yourself?'). Keep a diary if you want, or even just a notebook with bullet-pointed symptoms, moods, thoughts and behaviours. Put time stamps next to each point – there may be something significant in the timings, and having as much information as possible isn't going to hurt. They'll also probably ask you to fill in a survey (the PHQ-9 Depression Test, which you can find online) that asks you about these feelings and how you've experienced them over the past few weeks.

You also need to be prepared for the eventuality that your doctor may obstruct your access to services. There are lots of reasons why this might happen. Doctors are often stretched, and so are mental health services, so they may not want to recommend you for something that's already oversubscribed if they're not sure that you're a top priority. Appointments can be incredibly short – sometimes just five minutes long – and getting across a meaningful point about your mental health in that time can be tricky.

It could be, however, that you're just unlucky enough to have a doctor who doesn't take mental health as seriously as physical health. I've had a mixed bag – some incredibly understanding, some less so. Other friends have been totally incredulous at my experiences, having only come across helpful, empathetic GPs. There's no way to tell who or what you're going to get, so it's good to steel yourself just in case. Maybe this makes me a pessimist, but I like to think of myself as a completist: there is no worry I will not collect, ruminate upon and then prepare for. Sometimes this can pay off.

Be prepared to feel uncomfortable and sad and maybe burst into tears unexpectedly at a perfectly innocuous question. Be prepared for it to be, potentially, a draining experience.

Don't feel you have to know exactly what you want from an appointment, though. It's easy for me to say, 'I need to go to the doctor to change my medication' because I've been certifiably mental for ten years. I've been through it all: the nerves, the misdiagnoses, the medication and the therapy and the breathless, fruitless attempts to convince stony-faced doctors. You may not be at that point yet and that is totally OK. Maybe have a think about what it is you're after: do you want medication or therapy? Do you want to be diagnosed immediately, or do you want to be referred to mental health services? It's OK to not have a definite answer to any of these questions, but they are worth thinking about.

Know what you're talking about

It's easy to feel intimidated by medical professionals, but always remember that you are the expert on your own life. You know how you feel; you know what your symptoms are. Write them down. Look them up. Self-diagnosis is often frowned upon but it's important to understand yourself, to understand how your janky emotions or lack of coping could potentially fit into broader diagnostic spectrums.

Stand your ground

You might be lucky enough to see a good doctor who believes you and sincerely wants to help you. You might not. It can be almost impossibly hard if that's the case, but try not to let them argue you into submission. You are ill. You need help. And they are the gatekeeper to this help. Don't let them block access because of their own prejudices.

Don't get disheartened

One bad experience can leave a perpetual bad taste in your mouth, and I still feel dread every time I have to see a doctor about my mental health because my previous experiences have been so bad. Don't let this happen. If one doctor doesn't help, book an appointment with a different one. Change surgeries. If you can, pay to see a private psychiatrist. Research local therapists – they can't diagnose you, but they can offer advice and support throughout the process and may help you develop the emotional vocabulary to approach diagnosis again.

This can be the hardest part. The absolute despairing lows I've experienced after being knocked back by doctors have been awful. I've felt ignored, unimportant, small. It's vital that somehow you get past it in order to access help. A good thing to remember here is that *most doctors are genuinely there to help you*. You may come across someone obstinate and difficult and contrary, but the vast majority of medical staff are well meaning and well equipped to deal with whatever issues you have.

Remember you are not your diagnosis

Think of yourself as one of those women you see in adverts for tampons. There they are, rollerblading and ice-skating and swimming with gay abandon, not giving a single thought to their period. Your diagnosis is the same. It must not define you.

I spoke to a recently qualified doctor friend while writing this book, and our chats have given me somewhat more confidence in mental health care on the NHS. Her training was comprehensive – at least eight weeks of psychiatry training including a placement, either with a hospital-liaison psych team, who see referrals from other teams, or a placement in a psychiatric unit. She also did four weeks of child and adolescent psychiatry as part of her course, eight weeks of lectures in psychiatry and four weeks in a female in-patient unit. She also elected to do an extra short course on cognitive behavioural therapy (CBT), which was available to all her coursemates.

'We cover lots on depression, bipolar, schizophrenia and personality disorders such as borderline and schizoaffective disorder, and also cover alcohol and drug addiction,' she told me. 'I think there's generally a bigger focus on it now, and the importance of mental health more generally.'

Her advice echoes mine: if a GP is being unsympathetic or unsupportive for whatever reason, whether it's time constraints, miscommunication or just a poor attitude to mental health, 'don't waste your mental energy on figuring out what happened'. Find a new GP – in the same practice, or another if you have to – and try again. 'Don't forget that your problems won't be solved that day,' she says. 'It's the beginning of a very long journey.'

The Benefits of Diagnosis

I've been kind of hard on diagnosis, but that's not to say that I don't think it's valuable – as I've said, it is. I'm just wary of the dangers of becoming completely subsumed by it. But in a practical sense a diagnosis provides a number of valuable things.

Firstly, it is the initial step in accessing help. What that help might be may not be completely apparent to begin with. Will you need medication, for example? Will you go for therapy? Will you be referred to other services within the NHS, or will you take your diagnosis to a private therapist or mental health worker? Having a diagnosis makes all of this easier; and in the case of the NHS, it actually makes it possible full stop. Many mental health services on the NHS are wrapped in intractable loops of bureaucracy, and an initial diagnosis from a GP – even if it changes further on down the line – gives you access to these services in a way that is just not possible without a referral. When I turned up at the west london hospital mental health trust sweating and weeping and close to suicide, they wanted to help, but they couldn't *do* anything practical for me beyond sitting me down, talking to me and trying to calm me down. They needed a referral from my GP, which, of course, I didn't have at that point.

A diagnosis not only allows you to get to these services but also to navigate the system to maximum advantage. A diagnosis of bipolar is very different from one of severe anxiety or depression, for example, and your route through the mental healthcare system will be entirely different too.

Diagnosis can also help you relate your condition to other people. There's much more on this later in the book, but in brief, sharing your diagnosis can be an easy way of helping the people around you to understand and conceptualise what it is that you're going through. Obviously, it's not always as simple as that; sometimes people have misconceptions of what particular mental illnesses 'mean' – sometimes they'll have a whole bunch of unhelpful stereotypes whizzing around their brains, but most of the time they will not.

My experience has been generally positive; when I tell people I have bipolar they mostly understand what I mean by it. When they don't, I can explain it to them in broad terms, using both my own experience and my wider knowledge of how the condition manifests in other people.

And diagnosis can also help you understand your own condition. Even now, nearly two years after my initial diagnosis of bipolar, I'm still fitting things together and understanding how patterns of behaviour have affected me throughout my life. I do this mainly through the lens of, and with the help of, therapy, but sometimes things just click. I hadn't realised until about two months ago, for example that the general cycle of my moods changes with the weather. I interviewed someone with bipolar – a musician I admire – and when describing how his condition manifests itself, he mentioned offhand that when it gets warmer he's more likely to become manic. It was only then that I thought about the timings of my own psychotic and manic episodes and my depressions, and realised, despite having lived with bipolar for nearly ten years, that it has been, broadly, the same for me. It was discussing diagnosis – discussing a very specific condition, rather than 'mental health' in the abstract – that helped me on my way to this revelatory and very obvious realisation. This is the kind of conversation that diagnosis can foster – healthy, useful and practical.

CHAPTER 2

SELF-CARE

I was three weeks into my breakdown before I made an effort to do something about it. I was constantly hearing a dial tone that faded in and out of my head in bed, on the Tube, in Tesco. Sometimes it was a barely-there whisper, at others it would drown out almost every other noise. It started to dictate the rhythm of my conversation, the music I listened to. It had become a comfortable hum behind the dreary monotony of suicidal depression, something that actually perked my day up a bit because it felt so tangible.

Of course, it wasn't the first time I'd gone mad. It wasn't even my first 'nervous breakdown' (the euphemistic term my parents prefer to 'psychotic episode'). But it was probably the first time I was so acutely aware of the fact I was having one. Weirdly, it wasn't the auditory hallucinations or the self-harm or the countless suicide attempts that made me realise how fucked-up I had become; it wasn't even the constant presence of a gaping, cavernous emptiness that sometimes crushed my chest so hard I couldn't breathe, nor the fact that, for two weeks, my diet had mainly been composed of as much booze as I could afford or stomach and one small packet of sushi a day. It was realising how messy my flat had become.

The floor was covered in clothes I hadn't washed in weeks and weeks – clothes I hastily sprayed with perfume before putting them back on to go to work. Everything was fetid and stale and had a sharp, musky smell that couldn't be disguised by the fragrance I was trying to mask it with. I would often catch a hint of this smell in meetings or at the supermarket, and it filled me with so much shame I couldn't make eye contact with anyone and my hands would start to shake. The shame was so potent because it was imbued with the sense that this was preventable; if I had only taken that shower, this wouldn't be happening. And shouldn't taking a shower be the easiest thing in the world? Don't other people do it without thinking? It was this sense of self-rebuke that, ironically, made it even harder for me to put any of this desperate desire into action. I couldn't imagine my colleagues or friends would understand just *why* I couldn't spend fifteen minutes a day in the shower. *I* couldn't understand it myself, and that made my paralysis even worse.

Added to all this, my drinking was by now out of control, and I no longer had the prescience to hide it; my floor was full of empty and half-empty bottles of beer, wine, gin and vodka. I had become particularly fond of a cheap brand of rosé wine – I don't know how I drank it, it was so sweet and cloying – and buying it became the only part of the day I would look forward to. I could never be without a bottle or two in the house, or I began to feel panicked. So every night on my way home from work I would religiously buy two bottles and set about drinking it as soon as I got in.

It went like this, without fail: I'd slam the front door behind me, dump my bags on the floor and immediately strip off, leaving the discarded clothes by the door. Then I would get into my unmade bed, still naked, and begin to drink the wine. There was no point using glasses or cups, as I'd only have to wash them up later (once, a fly died at the bottom of a glass I'd left for days and I had to throw the whole thing away), so I would just swig from the bottle, not stopping until I passed out two hours later at around 9pm. It was kind of like when you're at university, strawpedoing a bottle of Lambrini, but with slightly fewer teenage boys dressed in bedsheet togas and marginally more existential dread.

Some of these bottles were inevitably knocked over during nocturnal stumbles to the toilet to pee or be sick, and obviously I never bothered to mop up any of the resulting alcohol spills. As a consequence, much of the floor was gummy, and in some places fluffy from the combination of stickiness and fibres from my clothes. There were probably forty or fifty bottles of wine, beer, vodka, gin and cider on the floor, stuffed down the side of the bed and on the windowsill. Some of them even had fag ends in them; it was so clichéd that it would have been funny if it wasn't so utterly, horribly tragic. I once texted a photo to my best friend – a friend who was well aware of all of my problems and who had plenty of her own – and even she was shocked. 'Fucking hell, Emily', she texted back. 'Fucking hell.'

There were unread books littering the floor too, and I found it darkly hilarious that most of them were about mental health. It looked like the set from a bad film; Sylvia Plath books next to empty bottles of vodka and packets of cigarettes. If I'd got the right filter and a good crop tool I could even have Instagrammed it and copyrighted the Sad Girl aesthetic once and for all.

Meanwhile, blood spattered the bed to the extent that it

looked like someone had been stabbed in it. It wasn't all that easy to distinguish between blood from self-harm and menstrual blood, which I had allowed to seep into the sheets. This was far better than buying pads or tampons; to do that, not only would I have to leave the house, but I might actually have to look someone in the eye. Both of these scenarios were simply out of the question. I kept telling myself every day that I would definitely change the sheets that night. But I didn't. And in the end my sheets were so hard with blood that I just put them in a plastic bag and threw them in a public bin. I was too scared to put them in my building's communal bin because I was convinced that someone would see them and I'd be investigated for some kind of horrible murder or Satanic ritual.

All this had gone on for so long that it had become kind of normal to me. I wasn't seeing anyone, choosing to communicate with people online instead of in person, so it wasn't even as though I could compare the way I was living with the clean, ordered life of someone sane. I was overcome with a kind of grim resignation that I could never be clean or functional, that this was just how it was always going to be for me. I knew it was gross, and I knew it definitely wasn't 'normal', but it was normal for me, and I didn't really care anyway. Even if I did, I was far too paralysed by depression, anxiety and fear to have been able to do anything about it.

And I'm not the only one this happens to, either. After I finally told someone how I was living, a friend recounted a similar story. She'd wake up every morning and move all her dirty clothes, muddy shoes and unclean plates from her bedroom floor onto her bed, telling herself that today she really would sort it out. She had to do it, or she wouldn't be able to get back into bed – right? Then, ignoring it all day, she'd eventually move it all back to the floor. This happened so often that eventually she gave up and slept among this weird, unhygienic detritus for three weeks.

For her, and for me, the mess kind of represented our horrible, oppressive mental state at the time. Of course, the majority of it was plainly because we couldn't function, but there was also another element, a more meaningful psychological significance. In the same way that self-harm can be a physical expression of pain, anger or despair, the pile of clothes on my friend's bed or the pile of bottles on my windowsill became a tangible metaphor for the depths of the low we felt and how little we thought of ourselves.

The turning point came one night around Christmas, when I brought someone I was dating back to the flat on a whim. I was a bit drunk (of course) and had thought that the flat was only a little bit messy. It was only when we got back that I realised how truly, horrifyingly terrible it was. I saw it all through his normal-person eyes, rather than my insane ones, and I suddenly got the horrible feeling that I might not be as OK as I had been convincing myself I was.

Panicked, I made him sit in the living room while I went into the bedroom. I think I may have even used the phrase 'freshen up'. What this actually meant was hastily shoving everything from the floor into my wardrobe, and drawing the curtains so the gross, boozy windowsill was hidden. In the morning he innocently drew back the curtains to let the morning light in and a look of unreserved horror passed over his face. I can only imagine what he would have thought if he'd seen the terrible muddle of spilled alcohol and dirty clothes that lay undiscovered in the wardrobe. As it was, he cleared the empty bottles for me as I sat watching him, absolutely on fire with mortification and wishing I could either transport myself literally anywhere else or, more pressingly, be a different person entirely.

Although the date wasn't important, the way it made me feel was. It made me realise how abnormal and dysfunctional I had become – and when I say dysfunctional, I mean it in the most basic terms. I was simply not doing any of the things a person needs to do to survive, let alone be happy. I can't say the incident 'cured' me, or even proved too significant a catalyst, but it definitely nudged me towards a mindset where I could start sorting my life out again. I didn't want to be constantly ashamed of myself or the way that I lived. I wanted to be able to bring friends and partners back to my house without having to embark on a two-day operation to conceal my dirty crockery. And after a shitty day at work I wanted to be able to get into a bed that was clean and fragrant and not full of empty bottles and blood. I wanted to actually have clean clothes.

It got better eventually. My laundry basket emptied, I threw away the rubbish, I scrubbed and hoovered all the floors. Starting to clean my flat is the first sign for me that my depression is lifting – the first reminder that I can be happy and capable, or at the very least that I can *cope*. But I also know that, one day, I'll find myself unwashed and exhausted among a pile of bin bags once more. I have no doubt that it will happen again.

What the experience really illustrates to me is the huge gulf of understanding between the abstract and the actual when it comes to depression. 'Depressed' is a word that has come to mean something quite different from the medical definition. It evokes something more passive than 'sad' and maybe sits more closely to 'melancholy'. William Styron described the word as a slug that has 'slithered innocuously through the language, leaving little trace of its intrinsic malevolence and preventing, by its insipidity, a general awareness of the horrible intensity of the disease when out of control'. This is true both for the emotional sides of illness and the physical realities of it; but the conversation often swerves the reality of actually living, day to day, with an illness.

As has been very clearly demonstrated by my own experience, depression can be fucking *disgusting*. You often hear about people not being able to get out of bed, or not showering for a while, or letting their room get really messy, but for me these are just comfortable euphemisms that give the reality of my life with depression a socially acceptable face. Depression is often thought of as a passive illness, characterised by lack of action, and in many ways it is. But lack of action doesn't leave you floating in a vacuum; it can leave you smelling like you live in a bin in a flat that looks like a shit Tracey Emin installation from the early '90s.

There are plenty of other examples. There have been times when my kitchen sink has heaved with multi-coloured mould, and I've eaten undercooked pasta with a cheese grater as a spoon because there was neither cutlery available nor a single chance that I was going to stand and wait for five more minutes to cook my dinner properly. I've gone days and days without showering – not even after sex, or on my period, although I had to go to work. At my deepest, darkest low, a used tampon sat in a kebab box on my bedroom floor for a shameful three days before I mustered the energy (and the stomach) to throw them both in the bin. Even then, it took me a while to take the bin bag out, its smug shine mocking my inability to move for two more days. I've put perfectly good forks and knives and plates in the trash because that seemed easier than washing them. Eventually, sincerely believing I would never wash up a single thing again, I gave in and bought paper plates.

Others have reported similar scenarios to me: sleeping in beds covered in blood, wearing stained and crusty clothes for weeks on end, peeing in vases or bowls or cups in their rooms to avoid going to the bathroom. One friend cried so hard she was sick, and then slept in her vomit-stained bed for four days. Mould has crept along their walls and onto their pillows, and they've slept beside empty bottles and half-eaten pizzas and dirty clothes. Once, a friend's neglected bin bag split and leaked onto the floor, the fetid juices rotting and fusing to the floor until eventually they had to be scraped off, bit by nauseating bit.

My manic episodes can often lead to the same messy results, but out of a pure lack of time more than anything else. If you spend thirteen nights out of a fortnight drinking, not going home for three days at a time and taking a small mountain of drugs while you're at it, you're probably not going to be totally on top of your cleaning rota. You probably won't have time to eat well, or do anything that requires more than thirty-five half-arsed seconds of fleeting attention. You might be one of those people who obsessively cleans when they're manic. I am not. Like my depression, my mania involves me inadvertently making my living space as disgustingly uninhabitable as it can possibly be. It's such an obsessive preoccupation for me that sometimes I feel like my whole life is a protracted piece of performance art about cultural conceptions of hygiene.

Some experiences are more extreme than others; to say

this is my normal life, or the normal life of someone else with mental health problems, would be disingenuous and reductive. Not being able to cope can be more low-key, less shockingly dramatic. Some depressed people can be perfectly functional – going to work, doing their essays at university or school, maintaining a brave face in public. But sometimes they secretly self-harm, go straight to sleep as soon as they get home or blow off their friends to sit wordlessly in the dark feeling utterly hopeless. They can't write like they used to, can't focus on work, they develop drug or alcohol problems, become incapable of using public transport . . . Or maybe they just feel like shit *all the time*. Despair isn't always explosive; it can be quiet and hopeless too. At these times, looking after yourself can be impossible. And this is where basic self-care comes in.

Self-care

Self-care is such a broad term that it can often be quite hard to define, and in many ways is so basic and necessary to a joyful existence that it can seem facile to isolate, list and actively attempt. What we already know, though, is that depression makes basic survival almost comically difficult.

What is Self-care?

It may sound simple and fairly obvious, but self-care is anything that can make you feel good, or at least better, in an emotional or physical sense. It's a deeply personal thing, including anything from 'simpler' tasks such as having a shower to more complex acts like taking up a hobby or working for a charity. I like to think of self-care as a means of reclaiming yourself and rediscovering your capacity for pleasure as well as for basic acts of fulfilment. It's the stuff you do to make yourself feel content, basically.

In recent years there's been a lot of online discourse around self-care, and it is one of the best things to come out of online mental health activism. It gives people with mental health problems a forum to express themselves, and provides a supportive community for those of us who find it hard to love ourselves all the time and need inspiration and help in order to care for ourselves. There are scrapbooking ideas, useful lists, blogs with links to calming noise generators and DIY face-mask recipes and images full of positive affirmations. It's a great resource. Sometimes, when I'm feeling a little bit down, rather than earth-shatteringly awful, even reading these lists make me feel better, regardless of whether I act on any of their suggestions or not. They add a dimension of hope to my life; the idea that I can, and will, cope.

However, there is one thing missing from this discourse: it often neglects to deal with those times when you're truly incapacitated by your mental health problems. The basic stuff; wanting to be clean, and safe, and not suicidal. With this in mind, there are certain things that often come up when you research self-care. Perhaps surprisingly, considering that the contents are generally geared towards and written by those who have mental health problems, it actually reflects quite closely some of the most frequently heard suggestions that come from those without them: do some yoga, eat a healthy meal, read or recite positive affirmations, do something altruistic. And you know what? All these things make sense. Exercise is great, and so is eating well and being an active, engaged, positive person. They all rule, and are all excellent ways to maintain a healthy mind and body. But when you are truly low, they are useless and fail to deal with those times when you're totally incapacitated by your mental health problems. You're living in squalor and you've not left your house in days. You subsist on a diet of Frazzles and lukewarm beer. There is no way you're getting out of bed, or doing three weeks' worth of laundry, and there is not a solitary hope in hell that you're going for a fucking run. Maybe when you're stable and settled and feeling OK you can start training for that 10k, or totally overhauling your diet and making complicated, fifteen-ingredient quinoa recipes or whatever. But often, you're not going to be able to do that when you're profoundly depressed. And that is *totally OK*. So, you need strategies to help you when you feel almost unable to function.

Self-care 101: Fifteen ideas to help you get your shit together

So you feel like shit. You're in a really sorry state. What do you do? Well, here are the most basic acts of self-care, mainly addressing physical sensations and physical safety. They're extremely rudimentary, but they matter, because whatever makes you feel good – or even just slightly less bad – is valid and important and, most of all, powerful.

- **Open your curtains**

  Doing this always makes me want to hiss like a vampire at the sunlight, but after a while it does actually make me feel more like a human being. Bonus points if you have an untidy windowsill and you tidy it up at the same time; double bonus points if you also open your window.

- **Get some air**

Going outside for a bit is the ideal here, even if it's for five or ten minutes. But if you can't manage that – which is totally OK, by the way – opening a window will do. Breathing in some fresh air will make you feel slightly better, and it has the benefit of making your house, flat or bedroom smell or feel a little fresher too.

Being able to actually get outside is slightly better even if you're wearing some kind of weird jumper/pyjama bottoms/coat/scarf combo that makes people look askance at you. But otherwise, just sit by your window and breathe deeply and rejoice in the fact that your room will probably smell slightly less like a rubbish dump when you're done.

- **Have a shower or bath**

A lot of self-care guides tell you to focus on your shower or bath in a meditative sense. Focus on the sensation of the water falling on your skin; really breathe in the scent of your soap. This can be incredibly relaxing, but for me the pleasure is mostly derived from the fact that I no longer smell like a fetid pile of garbage.

If possible, use bubble bath or a nice shower gel. You can get all kinds of fancy ones that cost loads, and which are lovely, but cheaper things work just as well. Lush is my go-to for this; I like to keep a bunch of their bath bombs and bubble bars in my bathroom cabinet for Emergency

Sad Baths. They smell good, they make your skin feel nice, you can sit for an hour or two getting pruny and watching bad TV on your laptop. At the very least, it can get you through a horrible hour; at best, it can feel almost transcendentally pleasurable to have warm water on your skin.

Wash your face

Nothing fancy – just some soap or cleanser and warm water. Again, if you can afford something more indulgent that's great, but it's more about rubbing the grime off your face.

If you're a make-up wearer who fails to remove it when you're depressed, do this. You will look marginally more fresh, even if you don't feel it.

Get dressed

I sleep naked, so this is often a very literal step for me. But if you're sat in pyjamas, don't feel like you have to put on something fancy. Just change from 'night pyjamas' to 'slightly cleaner day pyjamas', or put on an old T-shirt. Just change it up. I'm not sure why this works but it really does, and several independent people have relayed back to me during the writing of this book that they have a night-pyjamas-to-day-pyjamas ritual when depressed, so it clearly can help.

This works extra well if you buy yourself a whole load of cheap but very comfy PJs – you can get them in high-street shops for about £5 a go, so a job lot of three or four pairs means you'll always have something soft and nice and comfortable to wear. I like to gift pyjamas to friends when they're feeling depressed: something clean, soft and relaxing can make the physical discomfort of being miserable a little easier to bear.

- **Drink a glass of water**

Fun fact: many of the symptoms of dehydration resemble those of anxiety or depression. You may already be experiencing dizziness, light-headedness, exhaustion or an increased heart rate, which dehydration exacerbates or produces itself. Drink some water! It's not going to stop you feeling like shit, exactly, but it can help with some of the more horrible physical side effects. Drinking lots of water has innumerable other health benefits too, which can offset some of the physical side effects of depression. I also find that drinking lots of water is a key factor in my skin not looking terrible (yes, you still get spots when you're twenty-five – they lied to me too), which makes me feel marginally less like a terrible, ugly, amorphous blob. Plus, drinking more water means getting up to pee more, so your days spent lying in bed will at least be punctuated by trips to the bathroom. Scenic!

- **Stretch**

The best thing about this one is you don't even have to get out of bed to do it if you can't or don't want to. There are all sorts of yoga stretches you can do lying down/in your pyjamas/in bed – just Google them. For me, stretching my whole body out – my arms and legs and feet – can help me feel slightly more awake and alert and alive, and can remind me that the huge lump of meat that is my currently useless body actually does have the capacity to move and feel free and joyous.

- **Write a to-do list**

This doesn't have to be complex or full of challenging things. Think of it more as a daily-routine to-do list. Decide what you want to prioritise every day – getting out of bed before a certain time, having a shower, putting some clothes on – and put it on your list. Even if you're only doing very few very small things, ticking them off makes you feel productive and positive. Adding tiny, seemingly inconsequential things to my to-do list has been one of the best things I've ever done for my mental health; maybe I can't go for a run, but can I reply to an email? Yes. I've ticked off one thing; I feel more like a person who is capable of doing things.

Don't worry about the bar being set low and *do not worry if you don't complete it.* It is a work in progress, not a set timetable, so don't panic if you manage only one, or even none of the things on your list. Making a list is an achievement in itself, so you've done one thing already.

- **Tidy your immediate surroundings**

The phrase 'tidy house, tidy mind' is anathema to me, considering that I'm a pretty messy person at the best of times. I will grudgingly accept that there is a small amount of truth in it, though.

When I say try to tidy up, I don't mean doing a huge, deep excavation of your drawers and cupboards, or scrubbing things for hours and hours. What I mean is: tidy your bedside table. Clear things off your windowsill. Get rid of the small pile of clothes at the bottom of your bed. Hang up two or three of the pieces of clothing that are on the floor. Take the bins out. Even if what you're doing is collating the mess – putting it all into one pile, for example – you're doing a good job. You're making it slightly easier for future you – who will, as you know, absolutely be less depressed – to clear things up.

When I cleaned up five or six of my collection of fifty wine bottles, it helped clear my mind a little bit, even though it was a tiny and insignificant dent in a much larger job. It made me realise that the task, and, by extension, the depressive rut I was in, was actually conquerable. It was still a disgusting mess, but it was 1 per cent less of a disgusting mess. It helped; I felt a brief glimmer of what probably wasn't hope exactly, but something vaguely related to it.

Fill a bag with rubbish

Just one tiny supermarket bag will do. Chuck whatever is on the floor or in the bottom of your bag in there, or empty the fridge of gross, rotten food. Are there things in your drawers that you never use? Bin them. Receipts in your wallet or your coat pockets? Bin them. Get rid of lots of very tiny things; or, if you can, try to do something bigger and fill a whole bin bag.

Smell something good

Perfume, body lotion, incense, those fancy aromatherapy oils, garlic bread . . . Whatever. This feels really nice on a very basic level, and is also great for dissociation or anxiety because it physically grounds you. If you're having a panic attack, for example, a familiar or calming smell can drag you back down to a physical reality in which you can deal slightly better with what's happening.

It's all personal, of course, but some essential oils that can be good are lavender (smells like your grandma, probably, but is super calming), peppermint (which might invigorate you) or orange (which can also calm you down). I now have an essential-oil burner which I use when I'm down, as well as about a million scented candles, which (if I can be bothered to light them when I'm depressed) do make me feel something other than total sensory and emotional apathy. They also look nice, especially if you're lying in the dark, which provides an extra visual treat. (But please don't fall asleep and burn your house down.)

- **Eat something**

It's so easy to slip into not eating when you're really down. I often fail to eat when I'm depressed because it means either effort or money, both of which are likely to be in fairly short supply. I end up either drinking myself to sleep, unfed, or ordering a horrible takeaway.

We all know that it's probably best to eat healthily – eating well can make a difference to the way that you feel emotionally and physically. But fuck it. If you're super depressed and you want to order thirty pounds' worth of pizza and eat it alone in bed, then do it. The likelihood of you getting up and making a 16-ingredient stir fry with kale and beansprouts is fairly low, so just make sure you're eating *something*. (Plus, a slice of pizza with mushrooms on it is definitely one of your five a day.)

- **Move**

Guides to depression always bang on about exercise, which is great when you're stable, but less so when you're so low you can barely move your head to look out of the window. Do something small: walk to the end of your road and back, or up and down some stairs a few times, or do ten jumping jacks and lie back down again – something manageable that will make you feel slightly more energised but isn't Sisyphean in its impossibility.

You can even just shake your arms and legs a bit in bed, or get out of bed and walk around your room twice. You might find that once you've started moving you want to carry on; it's actually propelling yourself out of inaction in the first place that's the hardest part. At the very least, getting up and moving and it being terrible means that getting back into bed will feel incredibly relieving.

- **Talk to someone**

Talking to other people is probably the thing that I rely on most when I'm depressed. It doesn't have to be a deep conversation about the state of your mental health; it can just be a really laid-back chat with a friend or family member or someone online. Twitter, Reddit and other online communities are great for this because you're under no obligation to talk about ~how you are~ and you can just talk about *Corrie* or sex or hummus or whatever. There are forums for pretty much anything online, and whiling away the hours talking about a thing you're interested in can be a really good way of distracting yourself from your own low mood.

If someone can come over to see you or you can bring yourself to go to meet them, even better; being with someone physically can really help. If not, a phone call or a fun and distracting WhatsApp conversation can have almost the same effect.

• Do some breathing exercises

It might sound like bollocks, but breathing exercises really can make you calmer, more serene and better able to face the rest of the day. They are especially excellent for anxiety and panic attacks. The classic – breathing deeply in through the nose and exhaling slowly out through the mouth, each to the count of five – generally works for me, but there are a myriad others. A quick Google for 'breathing exercises for anxiety' or 'mindfulness breathing exercises' should give you a whole host to try, so you can work out what works best for you.

Don't worry if they don't particularly help, though. I have several friends who swear that even the most focused regime of breathing exercises does nothing for them. They've definitely been useful to me in the past, so they're worth a shot. There are a bunch of breathing exercises at the back of the book if you want to have a go (see p. 215).

These tips aren't the be-all and end-all of 'Getting Better' (whatever that even means), but they can be a great way to get started. Why not think of some more to add to your own list? Entering them into a nice notebook can be another way of distracting yourself, doing something productive and looking after yourself.

It's also SUPER important to remember that you're not

always going to be able to do even the tiny things that you want or plan to do. If you can't manage to have a shower or get dressed, you've not failed. Try again later, or tomorrow. Be patient and kind with yourself.

This is basically the real key to self-care for me: self-congratulation. I don't mean you have to throw yourself a parade every time you get out of bed, but it's easy to dismiss small achievements as meaningless. There's a tendency to write off a shower or washing up as 'just things that normal people do', and to self-flagellate over your inability to do them on a day-to-day basis. But depression is fucking *hard*. Not only is it emotionally hard, but it's physically draining. It saps every single ounce of willpower from your body. It makes your muscles hurt and it fucks your sleep patterns, often rendering you stupefyingly zombie-like, unable to process even the simplest, most undemanding conversations. So if 'all' you've done is open your curtains, remember that you've achieved something. Go you.

Advanced self-care

So, you've had your shower and got dressed and maybe you've even started doing a little bit of exercise. You're no longer falling through an unending void of despair, and you're feeling able to look after yourself physically. But how do you deal with the emotional stuff? How do you try to maintain this level of coping and stability?

You've probably guessed it by now, but the answer is . . . more self-care. You need practical tactics to help you manage the transition, rather than simply promising to 'love yourself' and hoping for the best. (Although, of course, a positive mindset is helpful, it's hard to sustain if you don't have anything to fall back on.)

This is all about maintaining stability, and is about more than just surviving and trying to get out of bed. With this in mind, it's important to remember that the following list is likely to be challenging in different ways; emotionally tough, or maybe even just kind of boring. Because getting well can be really, really boring.

• Do your research

If you have a diagnosis, it can be useful to actually learn more about it. There are hundreds of books about mental illness, from memoirs and biographies to medical textbooks and self-help, as well as innumerable blogs. The benefits of these are twofold: not only do you get respite from the sometimes crushing solitude of being ill and feeling like you're entirely alone, you might learn to understand yourself and your moods better too. There is no such thing as knowing too much about your mental health problems.

This can also help you develop coping strategies, as you're likely to come across a bunch of techniques from different schools of thought, or read blogs or articles by people with their own suggestions on how to get or stay well. Absolutely cannibalise every piece of information you think could possibly help you, and log them all in a notebook, journal or online diary.

• Keep a mood diary

Mood diaries are a key part of cognitive behavioural therapy, and are often used in other therapeutic programmes. Their benefits are multiple: not only are you being more mindful of your actions, thoughts and behaviours, but you're also able to notice patterns that can warn you of a potential depressive or manic episode.

A mood diary works fairly simply: you just record the time of day and how you're feeling, and can add other details such as sleep patterns, alcohol or drug consumption and diet. Establish a scale for your moods from one to ten – this might differ depending on what condition you have. If you have bipolar, for example, a one may be suicidally depressed and a ten may be manic; if you have anxiety, then one may be calm and ten may be having a panic attack. For depression, one could again be suicidal, but ten could be feeling happy and stable.

There's an example of a mood diary at the back of the book or you can Google mood diaries and print one off. I keep one in a spreadsheet on my Google Drive, so I can update how I'm feeling when I'm at work or on the go on my phone. There are also online programmes and mobile apps that allow you to track your mood, but a good old-fashioned notebook can work just as well if you'd rather have something tangible.

- **Write an 'In-case-of-emergency' list**

Are you stable now? Yes. Will you be stable forever? Maybe not. So you need to prepare yourself. What are your first warning signs? Write them down (the mood diary will help). Who should you call if you start to notice them? Write their names down and their numbers too. Be prepared. Give a copy of the list to someone else – a partner or friend or family member – and tell them what to do if you need help.

It may also be useful to share your mood diary (or at least a rough, edited approximation of it) with someone you really trust. You may not want to tell them every detail of your mood – some things are private, after all – but keeping them updated with the broad scope of your mood can help. If you're about to have a manic episode, for example, someone else may be better equipped to notice and quell problematic behaviour (by taking away your credit card, say, or ensuring that you stay in a set number of nights a week). This obviously has to be done with clear, engaged and ongoing consent, however, so that everybody is clear on the limits of their involvement and you're not being forced to do things you don't really want to do or that aren't beneficial to your health.

- **Eat well**

It's really boring, but leading a healthy lifestyle does actually help. The Mental Health Foundation suggest that wholegrain foods and those containing zinc (meat and dairy products) and omega-3 oils (like fish) are linked to good mental health, as is a daily intake of fresh fruit. Nuts, vegetables and pulses also fill you up and make you feel less tired, and low-sugar diets can help control the genuinely terrible mood swings and energy crashes caused by high sugar levels. You can also take vitamins (I take iron, vitamin C and vitamin D) if you want to boost your diet, but do check with your doctor or health professional before you start downing eighteen multivitamins a day.

Cutting down on alcohol and caffeine is a good way of

maintaining a healthier diet, as they can both exacerbate (and sometimes even trigger) periods of depression and anxiety. Caffeine is a big one for me: when I cut down, it was an almost transcendental revelation. I'd have a coffee before I got on the bus to work, then one as soon as I arrived. I'd drink tea throughout the day, and sometimes more coffee, as well as Diet Coke and sometimes energy drinks. I'd started exercising a little more by this point, and eating better, so couldn't understand why I felt so physically awful – I'd wake up sweaty and groggy and feeling as if I was about to die. But as soon as I cut down, this stopped. I had a headache for a few days, but that was about it. Caffeine had been a huge and completely unnoticed drain on my mental and physical health.

It's not just eating *well*, as such, either. It's about eating regularly. Try not to skip meals. Plan in advance if you have to. Try your hardest to eat fruit and vegetables and drink lots of water every day (again, there are apps which can help you monitor your water intake and will send you periodic push notifications on your phone to remind you to drink more). None of this stuff will ever *prevent* you from becoming ill again, but it can help maintain a feeling of wellbeing and may help you feel more stable and better equipped to deal with things.

You also, obviously, should still eat chips whenever you want.

• Do some exercise

Again, this is one of those things people who know nothing about mental illness tell people *with* mental illnesses to do, and it's really fucking annoying, so I'm kind of loath to put it in as a recommendation. It will not cure you. It will never, ever make you Not Ill. But it can be quite a useful coping mechanism, and as we all know by now, exercise releases all kinds of awesome neurotransmitters that can contribute to good mental health. So it's not all bollocks.

Don't do anything you're not comfortable with. Don't feel you have to go to the gym every day or run a 10k. Just do as much or as little exercise as you feel is right for you. There are fat-positive and queer-friendly gyms and workout sessions across the UK, as well as women-only classes. There are also a bunch of YouTube workout channels that promote body positivity without any of the damaging, patriarchal bullshit that says men and women have to look a certain way. These kind of tutorials can be a good way to start your exercise journey because you can do them at home and you can find out what works for you. I also find it quite hard to go to the gym; once I'm there I'm fine (if a little uncoordinated), but getting up, putting on gym clothes and walking there is really hard for me to do. Home workouts are great in this respect because you don't have to face leaving the house.

BUT! But! It is very important to note that exercise is *not* a panacea for mental health problems and can be very damaging for some people: the obsessive counting of reps or exercising too hard because you feel bad about your body or because you're manic, for example. During one particularly bad manic episode, I would go to the gym twice daily for about two months, and was barely eating either. I became absolutely fixated on how much I was working out and how many calories I'd burned. I was ostensibly doing something good – vegetables! running! – but was inadvertently rein-forcing negative behaviours.

Oh – and if someone tells you that yoga will cure your depression, you have my permission to tell them to fuck off.

- **Sort out your sleep**

Mental illness often brings with it sleep disturbances: you sleep too much or too little, and you sometimes ricochet, caffeine-addled and groggy, between the two. Practising good sleep hygiene (which essentially just means habits that contribute to a normal, good sleep) can make a huge difference to mental health, so read up on it.

Here are some pointers that have helped me and lots of my friends:

- ► *Try* not to be in bed for anything other than sex and sleeping.
- ► Exercise a little more – this can really help.
- ► Reduce your caffeine intake, especially too close to bedtime. I try not to have caffeine after midday, but four hours before bedtime is reasonable and achievable.
- ► Try – try! – to get up at the same time each morning to establish a routine, even if you're still tired. This can be incredibly hard to maintain, however, especially if you work from home or are a student, so don't get too hung up on it.
- ► Try not to nap during the day (which I guess goes back to the first point – not getting into bed to do anything other than fuck or fall asleep at night).
- ► Keep a sleep diary. Note things like the time you got into bed and when you eventually fell asleep, adding

details of any alcohol or caffeine intake and how much exercise you took. This may not be a short-term solution, but in the long term it can give you some clues as to what helps you – and what stops you – sleeping.

▸ Try to make your room a nice, comfortable and comforting place to be. Mine is full of paintings and books and fairy lights, which makes going to sleep some-what more pleasant than when it was full of cider bottles and unopened mail. When I get home and go into my bedroom it's a calm, relaxing place that just *feels* pleasant to be in – which obviously helps me get to sleep.

▸ Make a to-do list before bed. This may seem a little spurious, but it can actually help. I can't count the number of times I've lain in bed unable to sleep, patho-logically worrying about whatever it is I have to do the next day. Writing down what you need to do – even if it's one of the very small self-care 'Get-up, put-clothes-on, wash-face' lists – can clear your mind a little before you try to get to sleep.

It's important to remember that these kinds of holistic sleep-hygiene tips aren't always effective. Several of my friends have tried all of these techniques with incredible enthusiasm and still found themselves unable to sleep. If this is the case, head to your GP for a chat because they may be able to prescribe you sleeping pills.

Go to therapy

There's a whole section dedicated to this later on in the book (see pp.201–6), but it deserves a mention here too.

Therapy doesn't always work; it doesn't always make you

feel good. But for lots of people, it's a vital part of staying stable and sane, and is certainly worth a try if you have things you want or need to work through. It can help provide a safe, calm space for you to talk about how you're feeling, establish warning signs and triggers and give you some respite from the rest of your (possibly stressful) life.

Join a support group

This is something a number of my friends have done, and they've found it invaluable. The main – and most obvious – point is finding a group of people who just wordlessly understand what you're going through. There's the increased support, a new network of people who can probably provide the most specific care you need – they've been through it themselves, after all – and there's a therapeutic element too, which can either act as an initial way in to a further therapeutic experience or add to one you're already involved with.

Support groups are available across the country for a number of different mental health conditions, and groups that are specifically for young people, women, those who are LGBTQ+ and more are also available, so you should be able to find somewhere you feel safe to talk through your experiences.

Set goals

What are your aims in terms of your mental health, both short- and long-term? What do you hope to achieve? Your short-term goals could be 'showering at least four times a week' or 'getting to bed before 1am'. In the long term you could aim to 'stop self-harming' or 'cut down on drinking'.

Isolate your goals and break them down into smaller parts. Tackle each part methodically and carefully and don't worry if you have to start all over again more than once. And though it seems overwhelming, one way to achieve this is through SMART goals.

SMART goals

Psychologists talk a lot about 'SMART goals'. These are Specific, Measurable, Achievable, Relevant and Time-bound (hence 'SMART') and are essentially structured in such a way that they can be achieved most successfully. Quite often, this approach is used for big goals like graduating or getting a promotion or something, but it can be applied to goals at both ends of the self-help spectrum. I like to use it when I'm feeling horrible and only feel like doing some teeny, tiny acts of self-care. The example we'll use here is taking a shower because it's probably the thing I have the biggest problem with when I'm having a bad time.

Here are six questions you can ask yourself when setting one of these little goals, and luckily they all start with 'W', so they're easy to remember:

- **Who** is involved? This is self-care, so just yourself. That was easy.
- **What** do I want to accomplish? Get undressed. Get into the bathroom. Shower. Get dressed again.
- **Where** is it? The shower, obviously.
- **When** do I want to do it by? By 12pm? By the end of the day? Whenever feels good for you is fine, as long as you set an actual time limit.

- **Which** things will I need to accomplish this, and what are the constraints? You need yourself, a towel, a shower and some willpower. Constraints are not wanting to move or get out of bed.
- **Why** am I doing it? To feel clean and smell great and probably feel like 2 per cent better.

Breaking it down like this, and breaking it down even further into steps (1. Sit up, 2. Get out of bed, 3. Get undressed, etc.) can make small tasks feel a lot less challenging. You've defined the parameters of your effort; you have a better idea of how much energy each step will expend. This can really give structure to your self-care and can make actually doing what you want or need to do a lot easier. If you know you've done four steps of a nine-step process, then you know you're already halfway there; there's no nebulous dread hanging over your head because your path is clear.

So, how can we use SMART goals to tackle a bigger challenge? In exactly the same way. Although it will take longer and may require harder work than the shower example, SMART goals are perfect for accomplishing more challenging long-term aims. This time, we'll use the example of cutting down on alcohol. This can be a vague and intimidating idea, but by making it specific, it can become much more manageable.

- **Who** is involved? As always, you're involved, but this time so are others. Let your friends and family know you're trying to cut down on alcohol and ask them not to buy you drinks or offer you a beer or glass of wine when you're watching telly at the weekend. Ask them to be aware of your goal and arrange meetings in venues that don't involve alcohol, like coffee shops or the cinema.

- **What** do I want to accomplish? We already know that you want to cut down on alcohol, but remember the 'specific' part of SMART. Decide how many units per week you want to cut down by, or designate several days a week to be completely alcohol free.

- **Where** is it? This is less relevant because it doesn't take place in a particular place, but it's best to isolate the physical locations in which you're most likely to drink – at friends' houses? With work colleagues? – and be mindful of these places.

- **When** do I want to do it by? Again, this is personal choice. Set a reasonable deadline for yourself to stop drinking, and go slowly. Don't be afraid to modify your expectations; if, after a month, you're only on two alcohol-free days a week instead of the three you wanted, adjust accordingly.

- **Which** things will I need to accomplish this, and what are the constraints? Things you need: support from friends, an app or diary to track your drinking and potentially guidance from a counsellor or GP. Constraints are the desire to drink, triggering or provocative situations (dates in bars, parties or having a bad day).

- **Why** am I doing it? To be healthier, to develop better coping mechanisms, to lose weight, to save money – whatever the reasons, note them down and keep them in mind.

Sometimes, you won't be able to do anything to defend yourself against the unstoppable forces of mental ill health.

Sometimes you will wake up one day and think that you're terminally fucked. But other times, if you try to look after yourself and you pay close attention to how you feel, you can just about stop the horrible, crushing onset. Even if only for a slight respite, it is definitely worth investing some time in.

CHAPTER 3

DATING

Mental illness can be a solitary thing. What defines it above all else is introspection: the analysis of every thought and mood and whim, the endless dissection of every feeling. It boils down to the profound, secret hope of every ill person: that maybe, this time, with enough analysis, they'll find that elusive, significant key that unlocks the meaning behind all the senseless misery.

This often means that much of the literature around mental health focuses on this too. It asks, 'How do you feel?' or tells you, 'It was so hard for me'. Very rarely does anybody tell you how to be not only in yourself but around other people. Or, when they do, there's a weird focus on love as the ultimate redemptive force – a way to thrive and recover outside of medication or therapy. Relationships (romantic or otherwise) are always the climax in these kinds of stories, the final chapter that sends you on your way with a huge dose of saccharine hope.

But this isn't really how it works. Believe it or not, many people with mental illness have happy, healthy childhoods and cool friends and a normal social life. They have partners, wives, children, whatever. And most importantly: the vast majority of these are pretty standard relationships. Boring, even. Very few of these people 'save' you. They're just there, going out for drinks with you and watching *EastEnders* with you and texting you dinner ingredients on their way home from work. They're not cinematically charismatic people who rashly sweep into your life with perfectly formed pieces of wisdom. They just support you quietly, sensibly, steadily.

None of these narratives actually describe very accurately how mentally ill people do relate to others, meaning that you grow up blissfully unaware of the myriad ways that it *will* affect your relationships. By relationships I mean every single one: your romantic relationships, if you have them, your friendships, and your family life.

In this and the next few chapters we will be exploring these relationships. How do you navigate the muddied, confused waters of relating yourself to others? And what is it like from their perspective? In other words: what is it like to love someone who is mentally ill, and how can you help them?

The first relationship we'll be looking at is one of the most awkward to navigate: dating.

* * *

Dating is hard. It's paved with heartache and unrequited crushes and the blurting out of gabbled nonsense in front of the unimpressed person you like. When I finally found myself in a conversation with someone I liked at work, whose head I had resolutely stared at the back of for a full three months, I answered an innocuous, 'So, how's your day going?' with, 'I am awash with existential despair.' She stared, confused and unblinking, back into my face. I then followed it up with a tiny, pathetic, 'Woo!' She sat down again. I continued to stare at the back of her head from my desk, in the full knowledge that she would never speak to me again. This isn't just me, right? This is how it is for everyone. This is what it's like to date. It's awkward.

But what is it like when, in addition to your inability to say anything even remotely funny or interesting to the person you're into, you have a mental health problem on top of it? How does that affect how you interact with them? How does it affect a relationship once you're actually in one? And, maybe most pressingly: how do you even tell someone you are, or have been, ill? At what point during the dating process is it appropriate to bring up mental health?

The pressure of not knowing when or how to let someone know your mental health status can be an additional and very valid source of anxiety. If you tell them too soon it can feel like you're setting the stakes too high, but if you leave it too long you might find that the person you're dating has offensive views on mental health, doesn't want to deal with it or just isn't equipped to handle it at all.

As a serial dater it's something I've contended with a lot. It's also something I've done badly a lot. You would have thought there was a finite number of ways to do this wrong. There is not. And I still don't know how to do it; I always seem to mistime it, or phrase it badly, and I think quite often in my haste to reassure my potential partner that it's not really a big deal I can come across like a wide-eyed, mad cartoon person who's not only completely insane but also in denial. My latest approach is to just crowbar in the fact I'm writing a book about mental health – the subtext is clear as soon as I say it – but most people do not have this to fall back on. (Although I guess they do say that everybody has a book in them, and I do absolutely recommend it as an ice-breaker.)

How Not to Tell Someone You're Mentally Ill

Let's start with some of the poor ways I've handled this so far:

Completely avoiding telling someone until it was catastrophically too late

Hey! I thought, after a month or two of relative tranquillity. I think maybe I don't have mental health problems any more! I think maybe things are going to be great and perfect for ever and I'm never going to have to think about this ever again. There's absolutely no point telling my new boyfriend about it is there? Nah. It'll be fine. I'll be fine. I'm fine.

It was not fine.

It turned out he was the kind of person who called self-harm 'attention seeking' and thought anyone with depression should 'pull themselves together'. After two dates, this would have been fine – I'd have just dumped him. After two months, even, I could have escaped from the relationship pretty much unscathed. After two years, though, it came as a horrifying blow, and one that precipitated the inevitable end of the relationship.

I'd kind of avoided talking about mental health with him; at that point I was deeply embarrassed by my psychotic episode, and tried to distance myself from it as much as possible. It was easier for me to avoid the topic and skirt around it awkwardly than to confront it – even to myself – and instead I chose to chalk up my breakdown to the stress of starting university, moving away from home and spending all my time drinking. I really didn't want to think about the possibility that it might be something that would continue to affect me for the rest of my life. Looking back, I can see why: I just wasn't emotionally equipped to deal with that. I was young. And I wanted desperately, more than absolutely anything, to be 'normal'.

What this was, in reality, wasn't anything even closely resembling 'recovery'; I was lying to myself (and everyone else) about what I wanted out of life and my relationship. I was pretending to myself that I wanted to 'settle down' and live in an advertorial dreamscape, like something out of a 1950s advertisement, in which nobody is ever ill or unstable or even remotely fucked-up. It also meant baking a lot of pies, which was probably the only positive to come out of the whole thing.

But, inevitably, we ended up talking about self-harm and suicide. It was two years into the relationship and we were in the pub. I'd had a lot of cheap red wine, and I was the kind of drunk where the world gently, nauseatingly spins and all you can taste is metal on your tongue and you're quietly spoiling for a fight.

'It's all just attention seeking, isn't it?' he said. 'It's just people who want to feel special: "Oooh, look at me, I'm on anti-depressants!" Just get on with it.' He went on to tell me about an ex-girlfriend of his who had gone on antidepressants after her dad had died unexpectedly; he complained that she lay in bed all day and wouldn't have sex with him no matter how much he bugged her. It was brutal to hear him write off what was clearly a traumatic experience for his ex- as her being 'lazy' and trying to 'avoid sex' – as if her depression wasn't about her at all, but was a punishment she had actively decided to enact upon him. I hoped, for her sake, that he had never said these things to her, although from his tone I knew that he probably had.

It was deeply painful to hear someone I loved insult me in a way that seemed so fundamentally and unfairly personal. It was also an important moment for me because the breathtaking gut punch of the statement hit me in such a way that it forced me to consider how well I really was, and how totally integral my psychosis, my depression and my mania all were, in their own ways, to my self-image.

We argued about it a lot that day and from then on. He blamed me and said that he wished I would kill myself already and just get it over with if I was so serious about it. There's no doubt that he was a dickhead about it, but I can't help feeling that if I had talked about my experiences earlier on in the relationship the whole thing could have been avoided.

Rule number one: it is definitely a good idea to actually, at some point, tell them.

Blurting it out on a first date

I was in this weird little bar, and I'd just got a great haircut, and I was on a genuinely brilliant first date. He was tall, good-looking (in a kind of dishevelled professor way) and the first person I'd met who had piqued my interest since the breakdown of my previous relationship. I was very invested in not messing it up.

And I was nailing it. There was lots of wine and I was pulling out all of my best anecdotes. Most importantly, he had *totally* checked out my butt when I went to the bar. So it was going pretty well, really, until this exchange:

Him: 'So, you know I have a son?'
Me: 'Oh. No. I didn't actually.'
Him: 'Yeah. He's ten.'
Me: 'Don't worry about it. *I* have bipolar.'

So, not only had I completely failed to acknowledge anything he'd just said, but I'd also equated his beloved child, the centre of his universe, with a debilitating and heavily stigmatised mental health problem. I think I felt like his child and my bipolar were both things that could and would put someone off, and that he'd somehow just issued a Dealbreaker Amnesty by mentioning his son. In fact, he'd just wanted to tell me a boring anecdote about a trip to the zoo.

Rule number two: don't compare someone's child to a mental health problem on your first date.

Telling someone during sex

Things you can say during sex: 'That feels amazing', 'Keep doing that', 'Could you stop leaning on my hair please?' We've all read *Fifty Shades of Grey*. We know what's allowed.

But things you should not say during sex? 'So, you know I have bipolar?' Don't ask me why this happened. Don't ask me about the chain of thought that led me to blurt it out like that.

Just remember rule number three: never say it when you are literally having sex with someone.

Never.

How to Tell Someone You're Mentally Ill in None of the Ways Outlined Above

There isn't much we can learn from my horribly botched attempts at talking meaningfully about mental health with people I'm romantically involved with, other than please, God, for your own sake, do not do it in any of the ways I've described. I think that might be because – and this is an extremely trite and predictable thing to say – every situation is so unique and nuanced that there are no hard-and-fast rules as to what to do. I would love to be able to say, 'Yeah, you should definitely say exactly X after Y number of dates,' but relationships sadly don't work like a PlayStation cheat code, much as I wish they did. You have to play it by ear, pick up on the person's vibe and try to work out how best to communicate it to them.

I can give you some tips, though.

Actually tell them

Yes, this is obvious, but it's important. I didn't tell my ex- and we've seen how that went. Even if they're the understanding type, it's best to tell them before you have an episode because you'll need to have a conversation about what you expect from them or what you might need. If they don't want to date you because they can't handle it, that's totally fine, but it's unfair on both of you if they're forced to make that decision while you're ill and will cause undue levels of stress when you really don't need them.

Be honest

You don't have to tell them all the gross minutiae of your illness, but it's best to be broadly honest. Detail the type and severity of your illness. Tell them how it's affected you in the past and how it's likely to affect your relationship. Don't sugar-coat it.

Offer them some advice

Later on in this chapter there's a guide for the partners of mentally ill people (see p. 76). Read this list. Plagiarise the list and add to it. Give it to them, and make sure they read it. They might mess up a bit – who doesn't? – but this way they can avoid major pitfalls.

Don't be too hard on yourself

Having someone decide not to date you because they can't cope with your mental illness sucks. It feels deeply horrible and unavoidably personal. But . . . *But!* It is far better for you to be with someone who is willing and able to help you with your illness, who will look after you on the bad days as well as the good.

* * *

Having said all of the above, there's the question of whether you should even formally tell someone at all. Does putting such a strong emphasis on a diagnosis lead to an unhealthy overidentification? I'm certainly more than my bipolar – I am not my illness – so why is it important for me to tell someone in such a stark, matter-of-fact way? Wouldn't it be better to wait for the subject to arise naturally, if at all?

In some ways I'm sold on this approach. But bipolar is such a significant part of my life, whether I like it or not, that it would be lax of me to not mention it, and probably kind of irresponsible and unfair on who I'm dating. Some people can deal with mental illness; some people can't. That's fine. But I like to give them the option.

It may also cheer you to know that a 2013 study* undertaken by the charities Mind and Relate found that 77 per cent of people actively told their partners about their mental health problems and just 5 per cent of them experienced a break-up because of it. A further 74 per cent of partners of someone with a mental health problem said they 'weren't fazed'. So you have almost nothing to worry about.

Sexistential Crisis: Sex and Mental Health

The squeamish among you can breathe a sigh of relief. I'm not going to go into too much detail about my own sex life here. My mum's reading, for a start, and also there's enough gross anecdote to fill a whole other book. What I will say, though, is that sex and mental health, as with everything else in my entire goddamned life, are linked.

The main issues are twofold. One: a lack of libido. Two: far too much libido.

---

* 'People with mental health problems say partners "not fazed" when told about their condition,' Relate.org.uk.

Lack of libido

This is probably the less problematic of the two issues, but that's not to say it's not a big deal. It can make you feel awful: unsexy, unattractive, guilty. It can cause relationship problems or arguments, and be the source of a not insignificant amount of self-hatred.

Lack of libido is a symptom of lots of mental health problems. For me, it's been most striking when I've been depressed. The mental health and relationships study by Mind and Relate mentioned earlier found that four out of five people with mental health problems reported that their sex lives were affected by mental illness, with lack of libido at the top of the list.

When I'm depressed, sex is just . . . not a thing. I expend half of my energy on thinking about how I wish I was dead and the other half just trying to stay awake and alert and alive, attempting to feed myself and get on the bus and not openly scream with despair while at my desk. What with this packed schedule, there's just no time left for sex, and no drive or energy. All I want is to lie in bed, look at the Internet, eat some bad oven pizza and sleep. I will very occasionally mastur-bate, but that's about it, and it's mainly out of habit; sex just does not factor into my mental landscape. As a friend told me, 'I don't *want* to have sex, so I'm not constantly thinking, I wish I could have sex. What I *am* thinking is: I wish I *wanted* to have sex.' And that pretty much sums it up for me.

If you have an understanding partner, your lack of libido should not be a big deal. Obviously, nobody should ever pressure you into sex, make you feel guilty for not wanting to have it or otherwise make it a problem. That isn't a mental health issue, it's a relationship one: however you feel, however you act, nobody should *ever* coerce you or try to force your consent.

Nevertheless, a libido that becomes dramatically lower is an issue in a number of ways. Your partner may feel rejected or confused by your sudden lack of interest in sex – they might think it's something they've done. This is only natural, I think. When I've been on the other side of the whole thing I've initially worried that I was the problem – that it was me who was suddenly unsexy or unappealing. It's important at this juncture to reassure your partner that the problem doesn't lie with them but with you.

Explain to them that you're feeling depressed and that it's not personal to them. If you need physical space in general, tell them that it's because of how you're feeling and that you still love them. If you're still OK with non-sexual touching, then express your affection that way. But don't feel guilty if you can't.

Probably most importantly: *do not feel that you have to have sex if you don't want to.* I get the desire to please your partner, I really do. Their feelings of rejection or frustration are hard to deal with, and you might feel that they're your responsibility. *They are not your responsibility.* You are entitled to not want sex whenever you want, mental illness or not, so don't ever feel like you have to compensate for your lack of sex drive. This goes without saying in any relationship, but it's incredibly easy to lose sight of it when you're low.

Chances are it won't be your partner putting pressure on you to have sex; you'll be putting pressure on yourself. I am here to tell you not to. Relationships are about so much more than sex; they're about intimacy and trust and understanding. You wouldn't pressure someone else into having sex. Why put yourself under the same strain?

Too much libido

The other side of the coin is probably less common: hyper-sexuality. This can be a problem in its own right,* but it's also a side effect of several mental illnesses including bipolar, borderline personality disorder and obsessive compulsive disorder. The broadest definition of hypersexuality is frequent or suddenly increased sexual urges or activity – so wanting, or actually having, lots and lots of sex.

Having a high sex drive is good. Having a lot of sex, if you enjoy it: also good. Regardless of your gender, if you want to go out and get it, then go out and get it. No judgement here. There is a point, however, at which hypersexuality becomes a problem. When I say 'too much libido' here, I'm not talking about pulling someone at the pub every weekend or dating a lot. I'm talking about damaging levels of sex: compulsive sex, sex you feel you have no control over, sex as self-harm.

I'm not going to tell anyone not to engage in this kind of behaviour. It would be hypocritical for one thing, judgemental for another. There are a few things I would recommend, though:

- **Be responsible**

  Carry condoms everywhere. And if you forget to use protec-tion, then use the morning-after pill if you're able to get pregnant. If you can, consider getting contraception you don't have to think about. The Pill is very handy, but things

---

* Efforts have been made to include hypersexuality in the DSM, although at the time of writing these have failed.

like IUDs or the implant can take away the risk of forgetting to take it. In any event, however, ensure that you have regular STI tests and encourage any regular partners to do the same.

- **Stay as physically safe as possible**

The very nature of hypersexuality means that you might put yourself into dangerous or risky situations – normal reason can leave you as you tunnel vision your way towards sex.

Always tell a friend or flatmate where you're going – text them the addresses of clubs or bars or people's houses. Ask them to check in on you via text or phone in the morning. Don't let your phone run out of battery; carry your phone charger with you in your bag and get one of those portable chargers. If you see a plug socket and you can sit near it to look after your phone, charge your battery as much as possible, so that you're never going to be left stranded without some way of contacting friends or calling a taxi.

- **Be emotionally vigilant**

I know from experience that it can be all too easy to act upon physical compulsions without questioning them even slightly. Some of that lack of questioning has, for me, been down to reticence: examining my thoughts, feelings and behaviour could potentially make me stumble across an unwanted revelation, and so I find it best to ignore them entirely.

There are lots of reasons why you might feel compelled to have lots of sex. It could be an intense desire for constant stimulation that often goes hand in hand with mania; it could be related to self-esteem; it could be related to past experiences. Whatever it is, and despite any potential unwillingness, it may be worth taking some time to examine the thoughts you have about your behaviour.

There are also specific therapies you can undertake for issues around sex. The British Association for Counselling and Psychotherapy have a 'Find a Therapist' feature* that allows you to select a speciality. You might not want to stop, and that's fine, but talking it through never hurt anyone.

What to Do If Your Partner is Mentally Ill

So, what if you're on the other side of all this, and you're in a relationship with someone who's mentally ill? Well, you're probably mildly terrified of messing up, and maybe you have absolutely no idea what to do. That's fine, though. Totally fine. Nobody knows how to deal with it, other than by practising – and even years of tears and fuck-ups and arguments don't produce a perfect, failsafe technique.

What you have to contend with obviously depends on what your partner has been diagnosed with and how their symptoms present, but there are a few rules that can be adapted to pretty much any situation.

- **Prepare for it to be hard sometimes**

    We all know that no relationship is easy, regardless of the mental state of either party. Even if you're both totally stable, you will argue and get on each other's nerves.

* http://www.itsgoodtotalk.org.uk/therapists

Sometimes people fuck up really badly, but when you love someone you forgive them. Think of it like this, with the added caveat that they're trying really hard to not fuck up and that it isn't their fault. It's horrible to see someone you love in pain, but remember it's probably worse for them. Be supportive.

• Don't take things personally

If your partner is too depressed to have sex, or so anxious that they snap at you, or they're manic and decide to go AWOL for a few days, it can be really shit. (See previous point.) However, it's not about you. None of it is about you. When I'm panicked I am the grouchiest, snappiest, most mean-spirited woman alive. This isn't because whoever I'm with is necessarily being a prick. It's because *I* am. It will sometimes hurt your feelings, sometimes make you angry, sometimes make you sick with worry, but remember: it is not your fault. And it's not their fault, either. They're just struggling. Appreciate that.

That's not to say they're not responsible for their behaviour. If they say something hurtful because they're depressed and lashing out, make sure you talk to them about it at a later date; being mentally ill isn't a free pass to be unapologetically mean. Chances are, though, that they already know what they did wrong and are likely to apologise anyway.

• Understand what you're dealing with

Read up on your partner's diagnosis – personal accounts, medical textbooks, articles and online forums. Talk to them about it: how do they feel when they're ill? What are their most, and least, common symptoms? Become an expert on what they're going through. Don't talk over them, explain things back to them or profess to know more than them because you've browsed Wikipedia for an hour, but quietly let them know that you're invested in your relationship and are willing to learn as much as possible to make it work.

- **Have a contingency plan**

Know what to do in case of emergency. Ask your partner which family member or friend to contact if things get really tough. Gather resources (books, music, bubble bath, whatever) that can help calm your partner down in a crisis. Read up on and understand which local authorities you can contact if you need to. Have your partner's doctor, psychiatrist, therapist or care worker's number if applicable.

The most important thing here, however, is that throughout this planning process you have the explicit consent of your partner to act on their behalf when they're ill. You need to talk carefully and extensively about what your remit is as a partner, what they expect from you and at what point you would potentially be overstepping your mark in terms of their autonomy. You need to look after them, sure, but you also need to allow them to look after themselves.

- **Listen**

This bit of advice is in almost every section of this entire book, so you're probably getting bored of it by now, but I repeat it so often because it is the single most important thing you can do to help somebody who is ill. Listen to them and what they need, and remember that they are the number-one expert on their own life. You might have worked hard to understand what they're going through, and learned more about their diagnosis than an actual psychology student, but you should try to defer to them and their needs. This might not always be possible – they might be delusional or in serious danger of harming themselves, in which case taking control is imperative – but most of the time it is. Quietly understand and listen to your partner, respect their wishes and support them. That's it. Easy, really.

Things Not to Say to Your Mentally Ill Partner

Messing up is easy. Saying the wrong thing? Easy. A joke that falls flat, a light-hearted throwback to an unresolved argument, a reference to an ex- . . . there's a plethora of ways you can piss off your partner. And this is most strikingly the case when your partner has a mental health problem that you're not sure how to deal with.

But never fear! I am here to save the day. Though I can't tell you exactly what to say – as we know, everyone is different, after all – I can tell you what *not* to say under any circumstances. Ever.

'Don't I make you happy?'

I have had so many relationships that have made me happy: people who make me laugh, who intellectually stimulate me, who are just *so much fun*. Amazingly, though, this was not a cure for my mental illness. I still got depressed. I still had delusions. I still had auditory hallucinations. I was not magically healed because I do not live in a whimsical sepia-toned romcom in which the appearance of an older man or befringed woman solves all of my problems happily and quirkily ever after.

Asking someone whether or not you make them happy essentially makes their mental illness about you. You're saying, 'You have a great relationship and a nice life with me and you're still sad? What gives?' Maybe you are genuinely perplexed. Well, me too, buddy. It constantly puzzles me how I can have a career and partners and a great group of friends yet still be wracked with despair on a regular basis. It makes me feel guilty and ungrateful. Don't make it worse.

Instead, ask, 'What can I do to make this easier for you?' It may be that the answer is 'nothing', or it could turn out that you can do something practical to help (see pp. 170–5 for ideas on how to look after someone, or read through the chapter on self-care for simple things to encourage your partner to do – pp. 30–61).

'Why don't you just go to the doctor/go for a run/eat better?' or other equally arbitrary and totally useless sentiments

I know, I know, this is well meaning. It's also something that *everyone you ever talk to about mental illness* will say. Your boyfriend's sister did a Pilates course after she broke up with her partner. Your girlfriend's mum told her that you should try acupuncture. All well-meaning advice that would probably work if you were just in a rut at work or wanting to get a new hobby. But you are not. You are depressed.

It's irritating to hear this sort of thing from a stranger, but they don't know you, after all, so you can just ignore them. When it comes from someone you love, though, it stings like a motherfucker. The implication is, 'You're not trying hard enough' or, 'There are things you could be doing to make this relationship easier to handle'. And even if it is well-intentioned – and in most cases it is – it isn't helpful.

If you really want to help your partner, do the dishes maybe. Take over the finances for a bit. Give them a hug. Buy them a nice treat. Just don't tell them to go for a fucking run.

'Is it my fault?'

Much like 'Don't I make you happy?' (above), asking someone if it's your fault is not going to help. Sure, if you've made a snide comment, or not done something they asked you to do or forgotten to feed the cat, their bad mood might be your fault. But their mental illness, which is a nebulous and inexplicable combination of genetics and biology, brain chemistry and experience? Not really anyone's fault. Ask them instead whether anything in particular is bothering them; don't make it about you – because it isn't.

'I wish things could go back to how they were'

We all wish things could go back to the way they were, pal. We all wish that things were normal and stable and boring, that the biggest issue in our lives was the milk going off or something. I too wish that my relationships were not constantly beset by obstacles haphazardly thrown into my path by my mental illness. I too wish that I didn't have periods of depression in which I struggle to even vaguely recall what it feels like to laugh. And I too wish that I didn't have manic episodes in which I hear a phone ringing in my ear all night or think that the traffic lights are secretly surveying me. Would it be nice if I could snap out of mental illness like I do a bad mood? Yes. And would it be nice for you too? Yes, of course. But do I want to hear about it? No. Do I want to be made to feel guilty for simply having a mental illness? No.

'We all get sad/anxious/overexcited sometimes'

It's true. We do. Most people feel anxious before exams or driving tests or even sometimes for no reason. But most people are able to get out of bed most days of the week. Most people's sadness isn't pathological. And not everyone literally hyper- ventilates at the mere thought of getting a train or going to a party.

There's a big difference between the normal spectrum of human emotion, upon which everyone is always sitting and the experiences of someone with a mental illness. And while you may think it's helpful to empathise with them – after all, you're only trying to show them that you understand what they're going through – chances are that if you haven't got a mental illness, it isn't. It's much better to ask them how they're feeling, get them to describe their moods and behaviours to you and just *listen* than to try to throw your own experience into the mix.

* * *

Dating someone when you're mentally ill can be hard on them, but it's also hard on you. There's a lingering sense that you're unlovable, that you're inherently broken in some way.

Other people seem to sail through life totally unaffected by paranoia or anxiety or terrible, vicious sadness – why can't you? That's not strictly true, of course; everybody has their own shit to deal with, but when you're on the outside looking in, it doesn't always seem that way.

This is what lay at the heart of my hiding my illness from my ex-boyfriend – why I hid myself behind cooking and cleaning, inside a deceptively perfect domestic life that I meticulously Instagrammed for my horrified and bemused friends. I was a television version of a normal person, desperate for it to really come true.

I've had a recurring nightmare since I was around six years old. I first had it when I was ill, sweaty and feverish and stuck in that weird hinterland between dream and wakefulness, and then more frequently as I got older. I still have it now. In the dream I'm scaling a wall. It's one of those plastic rock-climbing walls they have in activity centres, and I know that the reason I'm endlessly crawling up this wall is because I'm reaching for something. I don't know what it is – the dream never gets that far – but there's this desperate sense of urgency, the knowledge that my goal is tantalisingly close, but that for some reason I can't quite reach it.

Relationships have always felt a little like this for me. I look at other people enjoying stable relationships and I marvel. How do they do it? How have they reached the top of this seemingly unconquerable wall? And who am I? I'm the ghost at the feast, the villain in a superhero movie locked inside a perspex box. I'm Morrissey standing alone in a club in *How Soon Is Now?*

Even once you fall in love, it can feel just as hard. There's a line in the Netflix series *BoJack Horseman* (ostensibly a programme about a talking horse, but actually a dark and intelligent musing on ego, depression and fame) where the eponymous character tells a girlfriend as she leaves him, 'This is what always happens. You didn't know me. You fell in love with me. You got to know me.' This kind of sums up the essence of how it feels to be in love when you're crazy. I have pushed many, many lovers away because of my deep-seated and unshakable belief that to be ill is to be unlovable.

Friends feel the same. They say, 'I constantly worry my boyfriend will leave me because I'm mentally ill', or, 'I'm always on edge because I think she's going to get sick of me'. One friend told me that her relationship is the biggest source of anxiety for her during a bad episode – that even though her girlfriend is supportive and always has been, the doubt niggles away at her: she wakes up thinking, Will she leave me? How much longer will she put up with this? She deserves someone normal. Of course, her girlfriend was horrified when she found out how much she'd been worrying; she loved her unconditionally, after all, and had her own concerns, including, 'Am I looking after her well enough?'

I've had quite a few long-term relationships as an adult, and they've been largely good. I've mostly been with people who have experienced mental health problems, either first- or second-hand, and who are also very smart. So they've had both an intellectual and an emotional understanding of my problems and, with a few exceptions, they've all dealt with them fairly well.

But the point here is not to show off (although I am very lucky) but to illustrate that despite this – despite the fact that I've had lots of relationships with people who are engaging, interesting, funny, talented and successful and who think the same of me – I still feel like my mental illness makes me an inherently unlovable person. I'm not saying that all of the fun and intimacy I've experienced with those people wasn't real – the sex we had, the in-jokes, the gin-and-tonic-fuelled debates on trains or watching eight Louis Theroux documentaries in a row. They all happened, and they were all profound or fun or somewhere in between. What I'm saying is that mental illness has made me feel like all this exists on a precipice.

There's a trope in cartoons where a character is running through a seemingly endless landscape, and then suddenly smashes through a screen. The horizon isn't real, it turns out; it's fake – it's a painted TV prop. That's how I feel about being in relationships, no matter how serious or casual they are. My surroundings may be picture-perfect, but I'm patiently waiting for it all to fall down and reveal the fact that it's just a set. And the thing that will betray me, that will demolish it all, is my mental illness.

It's not true, of course. My partners have loved me unconditionally, and generally we've never bickered about anxiety or mania or depression. Instead, we've bickered about the fact that maybe they sometimes didn't pick their wet towels up off the floor, or because I'm so contrary that I can start an argument, convince them of my position and then become so annoyed they agree with me that I end the argument saying the opposite thing. But these things – the things that cause friction – aren't generally about me being mentally ill; they're about me being human and having flaws and quirks (and a super annoying personality).

That's not to say my illness hasn't been an issue in my relationships. It has. And in some cases I'd go so far as to say that it's actively ruined them. Paranoia has been especially destructive in that it often leads me to obsess over perceived or suspected infidelities. I lived with a boyfriend at university, and it's not an exaggeration to say we spent twenty-four hours a day together. Even if he'd wanted to cheat on me he wouldn't have had the chance – we were inseparable. Still, my anxiety wore away at us both, making me terrified of his every glance at women on the street or of him being 'too friendly' with a cashier. It would send me into spirals of fear and terror that took their toll on our relationship. Amazingly, these episodes all miraculously cleared up when I was feeling mentally healthier.

Self-harm and suicide have also loomed large in almost all of my relationships. Partners have hated seeing me hurt myself, feeling powerless and impotent in its path. It's caused arguments, huge rifts and ultimatums from some, while others have felt unable to criticise me or break up with me in the misguided fear that I would immediately go and kill myself.

My illness has made me push people away too – scared to let anyone in for fear that underneath my gregarious, outgoing exterior is a gnarled, broken person. It's like I'm a Russian doll that becomes uglier and more deformed as layer after layer of artifice is revealed. Why allow someone to see it? Why let someone see the real Emily – Bipolar Emily – when all it's going to do is repel them?

But it's a false dichotomy. I *am* bipolar. I *am* ill. And sometimes that manifests itself in ugly, unlovable ways. But I am also kind and empathetic, and my friends tell me I'm smart, and I always tell the best and most outrageous dinner-party anecdotes. There are plenty of things to love about me. And the same goes for anyone with a mental illness. The two things co-exist; one doesn't cancel the other out, and nor should it. People don't love us 'in spite' of our mental illness. It's just a blank, neutral fact – something that has no moral value, but just . . . is. The 'real Emily' isn't the one that I hate or the one that I like. It's all of me; it's the unique jumble of happiness and sadness and mania and depression and love and anything else you can possibly think of.

I always thought my life was predetermined – that I only had a few options open to me. Option one: be 'cured' of my mental illness; meet somebody and be happy and normal for ever, white picket fence and all the associated regalia. Option two: accept that I'm mentally ill, but somehow get and stay well through the magical, redemptive power of love. Option three: be myself; that is to say 'fully, totally mentally ill', and always be alone.

It turns out that I don't have to accept any of these options. And nor do you. Love can help, but it will emphatically not 'cure' you of your mental health problems, no matter how many twee indie films tell you that's how it works. And you don't have to be totally stable, or stable at all, to be worthy of love.

This is something it took me a long time to learn. And it is something that would have made me happier in myself a long time ago: the fact that you can be unashamedly mentally ill and still be truly, wholly loved.

CHAPTER 4

EDUCATION

'm not sure where the adage 'School days are the best days of your life' came from, but it's always bothered me. Throughout my childhood and adolescence the phrase haunted me – a ratchety old spectre that popped up at every desperate moment of weakness or isolation or fear. Is this how it's supposed to feel? I would think to myself. Is this *really* the best it's going to be?

University compounded these anxieties. Wasn't I meant to be out there, having fun? Falling in love? Or even – though this was fairly unlikely – learning? I wasn't sure where 'there' was, exactly, but I knew it was *somewhere*.

A lyric from a Smiths song tormented me:

> When you're dancing and laughing
> And finally living . . .

I had cherished it for years, repeating it like a mantra and, above all, secretly knowing that one day I *would* be dancing and laughing and finally living.

But I wasn't. I had the perpetual sensation of being someone on the outside looking in. It was like an endless walk home on an autumn evening. I could look inside other people's windows, look at the warmth and joy and comfort they had, but I could never get in, never play a convincing or vital part in their weird, impenetrable ceremony of normality. I felt like this every single day of my life from the age of twelve to twenty-two – *every* day, floating on the periphery of something meaningful or fulfilling, never quite managing to capture or even understand the essence of what made normal people tick.

So, in short: no, my school days were not the greatest days of my life. Neither, for that matter, were my university days. And while some of my unease and unhappiness was down to being a good old-fashioned weirdo, a lot of it was to do with my latent, and later my manifest, mental health problems.

I find it slightly bizarre that people don't talk about these things more: how utterly miserable school days are written off as a by-product of being a moody teenager; how the desperate, clawing hurt and terror and misery of being ill and alone at university are thought of as growing pains or homesickness or as 'failing to find your feet'. I talk to friends and colleagues and the same thing crops up again and again: 'I was so depressed I couldn't function', or, 'I dropped out because I had a nervous breakdown'.

And it's not just anecdotal evidence that reflects my experience. Study upon study show how many students – at both school and university – have mental health problems. A 2013 study by the National Union of Students found that 20 per cent of university students consider themselves to have one, while in 2015, university counselling services faced a 10 per cent increase in annual demand.

Many mental health problems first manifest themselves in

adolescence. According to the charity Young Minds, nearly 80,000 children and young people suffer from severe depression in the UK, and the number of teenagers aged between fifteen and sixteen diagnosed with depression doubled between the 1980s and the 2000s – so the problem isn't going away.

So, why aren't we talking about it more?

Well, this chapter is my attempt to do just that. To normalise the experience of abjectly hating school and university, and to quieten that internal voice that says, 'Maybe this is how all teenagers feel'.

School

How best to sum up my school days? Which carefully chosen adjectives would make the list? 'Boring' is definitely in there. 'Unproductive' is also high up. But 'arduous Sisyphean nightmare' probably sums it up best.

The fact was that I just didn't like myself on a pretty profound level, and was even more profoundly unsure as to how I could express that. So I tried to bury it: leave it somewhere cold and dark beneath layers of uncertain narcissism; somewhere it would wither and die. But trying to ignore it made it flourish. It thrived there, in the dank gloom of my subconscious. It grew stronger, wrapping its tendrils around everything I did, and especially around my throat, which would open and shut dryly, emptily. I even found it hard to speak, the strange and breathy croak escaping my mouth absolutely betraying the weirdness that was going on inside my mind.

Being unhappy at school is an experience that many people live through to one degree or another. People are bullied or they're not well-liked or they're just awkward. But what is especially difficult is the combination of the normal, common-or-garden variety teenage unpleasantness and the onset of mental illness.

I don't really remember when I first felt truly depressed. I think it probably crept up on me, no one catalyst setting me off. I do remember the first time I tried to cut myself (more on which later), although I don't recall being particularly sad around that time, or particularly desperate. I must have been, of course, because I don't know why else I would have done it. I was too young to really know about it, and my slightly too-strict mum wouldn't let me watch the kind of kids' shows that dealt with 'teenage issues' like self-harm. Maybe it just called to me somehow – some deep and primal desire for pain that manifested itself in a pair of blunt nail scissors. Or maybe I was just copying someone else who was struggling with similar issues.

But whatever the reason, the fact of the matter is that I was miserable all of the time. 'Sad' doesn't quite capture how I felt – 'sad' is melancholy. Sad is soft. Sad is gentle. Sad is looking out of a window wistfully. It's comforting in a way. What I felt was much more vicious than that, much darker. One of the diagnostic criteria for depression is 'loss of interest in things you once found enjoyable', and while it's indubitably accurate, the phrase doesn't really do the feeling justice. Depression feels like a brutal rip inside of you: this horrible clawing rawness that sucks every ounce of joy or happiness out of the world. The simple pleasures of life – a cold glass of water, a song you love, reading – are gone. In their place? Sometimes an endless chasm of ennui; sometimes a fierce and desperate rage. It is a black hole in every possible sense.

But not only was depression a viscerally horrible experience, it was confusing too. As I got older, around the age of fifteen, I started to piece together the way I felt and was able to tentatively connect it to the abstract concept of 'depression'. Before that, though, I was unmoored, with no way of understanding or conceptualising what was happening to me. I knew nothing about mental illness, serotonin, depression, bipolar disorder or even chemical imbalance beyond a vague recognition of what the words meant in a literal sense. These were alien ideas to me, not something I could identify with or something that I'd ever thought about. All I knew was that every day was like a real-life version of one of those anxiety dreams where you're endlessly falling: there was a dark expanse below me – one that I was rapidly and haphazardly flying towards – but there was no way of stopping myself.

A lot of accounts explain depression as something that happens *to* you. It's described as an animal or a monster or as a curse or spell. I see where these analogies are coming from, I really do. You're unutterably miserable. You don't feel yourself. You feel heavy and tired and drab; things you previously loved have lost a shine that shows no sign of returning. You can scan your partner's face for hours, desperately searching for that impossible inch of skin that will make you feel emotion again. You never find it.

Even more desperately, you don't want there to be something wrong with you. Mental illness means doctors and pills and therapy; it means you're broken. It means that something deep and innate and inherent has gone wrong. You feel small. You feel worthless. You want to give up.

So anthropomorphising it all seems natural. You think of depression as some snotty monster dripping bile into your brain and it seems easier. You think of a big scruffy dog sat on your chest, not allowing you to move, and that seems easier. It's easier because it means something else is responsible for your misery. It's not you, after all. You're not broken, you're just temporarily weighed down by this unknowable creature.

Thirteen and miserable: this is how I came to think about my mental illness. As I said in an earlier chapter, I never thought of my sadness as being something to do with *me*. I flitted between two mindsets: the idea that I was making a rational, existential choice and the belief that I was a victim, someone who was being mown down by an unstoppable force that had as little to do with my sense of self as any other external energy.

It was useful to me for a while I think, as I got to grips with what was happening. But in terms of getting better, and actually living with mental illness, the anthropomorphic approach was somewhat lacking. Thinking of mental illness as something that happens *to* you absolves your responsibility; it makes you powerless. If there's a black dog sitting on your chest, there's not much you can do about it. If there's a monster invading your thoughts, then what can you do? It's not about you, then, it's about them (or, maybe more accurately, it). Obviously, nobody thinks that there is literally an invisible dog following them around, but these abstract concepts affect the way we deal with things. Whenever I thought about how I felt, I didn't think of my depression as being anything to do with my conception of myself. Why would I? I was intelligent, engaging, a little shy, perhaps, but personable and friendly. I wasn't sad. I wasn't irritable. I certainly wasn't so blank, so devoid of personality. These things just couldn't be me.

But they were me. They were me from the age of thirteen to fifteen, from seventeen and well into my twenties. They were as much me as my intelligence, my love of books, my never-an-inside-voice voice were. Mental illness happened to me, sure, inasmuch as my periods of illness are temporal events, but it's also an inherent part of who I am. No black dog, no malevolent force. Just me.

That's not to say that my conceptualisation of my mental illness was the only justification for not getting help at school. I didn't seek help because what good would it do? And there were lots of other reasons too.

A lack of appropriate vocabulary was one. Linked, in a way, to my self-imposed victimhood, I had no idea how to properly express how or what I was feeling. I channelled my frustrated energy into self-harm, a fruitless exercise that plunged me deeper into a cycle of self-loathing that solved exactly nothing. The secrecy of it led me to retreat further into myself, speaking less and less about how I was feeling until I became a numb shell, a conduit only for boredom and the tinny sound of Smiths' songs leaked from cheap headphones. 'I need help' was not a thing I knew I even *wanted* to say; and if it had been, I'm not sure I'd have known *how* to say it.

Now I've been through ten years' worth of mental health care, I broadly know what to ask for when I need help, and am confident enough to stand up to obstructive doctors. At school, I was not. I was desperately, desperately shy, and once I'd been told by a doctor that I was just experiencing the usual trials and tribulations of adolescence (part of the problem being actually getting people to believe what I was saying), I simply shut my mouth and refused to ask for help again.

A teacher, informed by one of my peers that I was self-harming, took me aside once – and only once – and told me I should stop. 'You don't want your arms to be scarred on your wedding day, do you?' he said. He was probably relating to me as best he could (girls care about weddings, right?), but it didn't help. He never offered help again; I never asked.

That's not to say you shouldn't tell someone; you absolutely should. My experience was particularly poor, but it's not universal. A close friend tells me that her English teacher, who she is still in touch with, was instrumental in her recovery from an eating disorder. She reached out, and it paid off; she got the help she needed, and is now still recovered and happy.

How to ask for help from a teacher

It's far easier for me to say, 'You should ask for help!' than it is for you to find the nerve to do it. It is indubitably scary and can be hard to know what to say or do, let alone what kind of help you should be asking for. Sometimes a shapeless, formless terror compels you to reach out to someone, but making this terror tangible can be difficult. Nevertheless, there are a few things to keep in mind when you approach someone for help.

- **Arm yourself with as much information as possible**

  I've advocated this many times already, so if you're not bored of this advice, you soon will be. But, on the other hand, I am right (and it's not often I can say that with this degree of certainty)! It is imperative that you have as much information as you possibly can. If you can articulate it, write down how you're feeling. Make a list if you need. Are you finding it hard to sleep, or sleeping too much? Write it down. Has there been a significant change in your appetite? Write it down. The same advice I gave for visiting GPs earlier in the book (see p. 22) applies here.

Practise what you're going to say

If you think you're going to get nervous (as I did), then practise what you're going to say. If there is someone you can trust, practise on them. If you don't feel comfortable discussing it with a friend, then write it down or talk to yourself in the mirror. Yes, you may feel dumb, but you'll feel far less flustered in the long run. You might end up just blurting it out at top speed and include none of the elegantly worded phrases you'd rehearsed, but planning it in your head beforehand will potentially bring you the courage to do it at all.

Remember that they *want to help you*

Being a teacher is about far more than prepping students for exams; it's about providing young people with a healthy, safe and comfortable environment in which they can thrive and grow. Looking out for the physical and mental health of students is part of the job. When my teacher tried to relate to me by asking me to think about my wedding day, he was trying to do just that; yes, he did it badly, but he still tried. The vast majority of teachers are more than happy to help you, no matter how nervous you are about talking to them.

Which leads quite neatly on to a different question: can

your teacher tell anyone else about your problems? Mine asked for my permission to call my parents and talk to them about what I'd told him. (I did give him permission, but he never actually spoke to them.) Others' experiences may be different, though. A teacher friend of mine tells me that if a student is depressed and their teacher offers support, it usually does involve telling the parents and safeguarding officers, but it doesn't have to: 'I've had students tell me they're depressed, but their parents don't know, and to pass that information on isn't necessary and is down to personal discretion,' he says.

Self-harm or suicide, however, are different. Teachers are legally bound to let safeguarding officers (heads of departments, headteachers or support staff) know if someone is in immediate danger to themselves or others, so if you're currently suicidal or self-harming, then that information may be passed on for your own safety.

My friend also gave me some other pointers to things to remember from a teacher's perspective:

• Pick your moment

If you're too nervous to organise a meeting, ask your teacher if you can stay behind after a lesson to talk about what you've been learning. This can give you a much safer and calmer space in which to discuss your mental health, and nobody will know what you really want to talk to your teacher about. If anyone else asks, you can just tell them you're struggling with something in the lesson or wanted to double-check a note your teacher left on your homework; no need to share unless you want to.

- **Remember you're both totally unique and not unique at all**

Teachers will have dealt with students going through similar things to you, and will have experience in the processes needed to get you help. But a good teacher will also be able to recognise that everybody's circumstances are totally unique and will need to be managed in a different way.

If they manage it well, they'll ask you for more details on how you're feeling, and will then try to help you deal with your symptoms accordingly.

- **It's OK to try again**

If you speak to someone who couldn't – or didn't – help you, it's OK to try again! Keep trying until you find someone who can empathise and who's willing to help.

- **Speak up early**

My friend gave me the example of a student who found presentations so anxiety-inducing that they would happily bunk lessons for a week. If this is the case, or your mental health is likely to affect your performance in some other way, he suggests letting your teacher know as soon as possible so that they can help you manage it. They should be able to devise strategies with you either to cope with your worries or get extra credit in a different way.

This can also apply to exams. With the right timeline, exam boards will often give special dispensation to students with mental health problems or schools can take steps to ensure the exam process is as easy as possible. You probably won't get extra time (this is more usually given to students with special learning needs, rather than emotional ones), but you may be able to apply for special consideration in terms of your mark, or you could ask whether it's possible to sit the exam in a smaller room if you have anxiety, for example.

University – a Beginner's Guide to Survival

I truly thought university would be different. I thought it would be the place where I'd magically come into my own, and become the person I'd always wanted to be – both a magnetic femme fatale and a deeply serious thinker, someone who would hold charming and witty conversations with capital-I Intellectuals and have a series of breathtaking love affairs with European girls with fringes and men in horn-rimmed glasses. And somehow, despite this sparkling social schedule and intense programme of self-improvement, I would also get a 2:1.

What actually happened was that I spent a year getting very drunk every day, had a psychotic episode and then spent the three subsequent years hiding in my flat, too scared to leave the building. University served to both highlight and exacerbate my mental illness, to refine it to its purest and most fucked-up peak. I had no idea what I was doing. I failed exams, I skipped lectures, I alienated everyone I met. There's no better word for the whole five years than 'breakdown' – because my life was a terrible, broken-down mess; like a car that won't start with a horrible, noxious exhaust pipe.

Of course, university is not a homogenous experience. Everyone encounters unique challenges, whether studying for or sitting exams, romantic relationships or just day-to-day coping. And sometimes you won't even know about your mental health problems until you get there. My own, although pretty well established, took on a different form at university; this weird, shifting entity that was entirely new and unknowable. I knew I was depressed, but until I was at university I'd never had what I now know as a manic episode.

So, mainly because I had been so ostracised at school, university seemed to me to be a good place to start over. I had a few good qualities; I was empathetic, I was funny, I was smart. Surely I could take these qualities and get rid of all the background noise? I didn't have to be this awkward, insecure person my whole life? I later found out that I didn't (I'm certainly not that person now), but what I didn't realise at the time was that if you want people to like you – *really* like you – the best thing you can do is be yourself. Obviously, not everyone will like you, but that's not the point; the people who do like you like you because you are good, and because of that peculiar mixture of likes and dislikes you have, for your smell and your taste in books and the way you open your mouth slightly gormlessly when you're thinking. I did not know this then. 'Be yourself' seemed like a trite and facile self-help mantra. It seemed like some kind of joke.

Reinventing myself seemed like a good idea – the last version of me hadn't worked, so why not try a new one? Nobody at university would have to know what I was like at school; that I'd had bad hair or that my personalised Myspace URL was '/ilovestephenfry'. I would be cool, interesting, aloof. I would, most importantly, be popular.

I dutifully dyed my hair peroxide blonde and bought a whole new wardrobe – the kind of clothes other girls wore, rather than the Doc Martens and band T-shirts I had got used to hiding myself in. (There was nothing wrong with these things, of course, nothing wrong with being gym-obsessed and thin and provocative in my dress, other than the fact it wasn't me.) I stopped listening to the music I liked and pretended to agree with everyone else. This meant no more arguments about queer politics and feminism. No – instead, I would be *agreeable*. I would *acquiesce*. I would exercise *restraint* and *self-control* and all of those things that make you much smaller but altogether more palatable.

Most significantly, I started going out. A lot.

There are lots of things shy people don't like. Crowds. Small talk. Getting into the lift with someone they kind of but don't quite know well enough for it to not be awkward. And sitting smugly at the top of this list is the common thread that haunts an introvert's life: socialising.

Socialising is hard. It's boring. It's thankless, mostly. It's endless small talk with people you barely know and definitely don't like. It's forcing yourself to appear happy or jolly or interested in what they have to say. It's insecurity – hoping that someone likes you, but sensing that they don't. It's saying the wrong thing and painfully receiving a blank and awkward response from your conversational partner. It can make you feel tiny and small, but is also inescapably perched on the edge of a precipice that promises you that golden chalice: popularity.

When I was eighteen, I was shy. Incredibly shy. I was also a year ahead of myself at school, which meant I'd turned eighteen only days before my first night at uni. My peers had been going out for a full year, drinking in clubs and bars and pubs, but I was too much of a chicken to get a fake ID and did most of my drinking in my best friend's bedroom anyway, so 'going out' as a concept was pretty alien to me. But 'going out', of course, is a fairly integral part of your first few weeks at university. Get it right, I thought, and I would be guaranteed ongoing social success. Get it wrong and I would be the friendless loser I had been for the previous five years. Getting it right seemed very, very important.

Freshers' week is anxiety writ large: meeting new people, navigating a new place, living alone for the first time. Add to that drinking, and sometimes drugs, and you have yourself a pretty potent and overwhelming mix, mental illness or not.

I started drinking in Freshers' week in a way I had never drunk before. The most intoxicated I had been up until that point was my first ever drinking experience: New Year's Eve at my best friend's parents' house when I drank two glasses of eggnog, three glasses of champagne and a few shots of chocolate vodka, then promptly vomited. Not in the toilet, of course, but in the sink, the laundry basket, the bed and the floor. Great stuff.

University introduced to me subtle new nuances in the experience of being sick – mostly in the toilet, luckily, but also on a thrice-daily basis. First, a wave of nausea would hit me at around 6am, when I would blindly stumble to my bathroom to throw up. Dry-mouthed and anxious, I would fall back into a fitful sleep before lunch, when I would eat a sandwich and throw it back up. (On a good day, I had drunk little enough that I could avoid this mid-afternoon session.) My final stint would be in the evening, after I had got back in from a night out; if I was particularly unlucky, this nocturnal ritual would start before I had left the pub or club. Occasionally, I would make myself sick on purpose – if I felt a bit ill before I went out, for example. This, for me, was a delightful new variation, eloquently referred to in the early 2010s as the 'tactical chunder'. It meant I could then brush my teeth and get on with the rest of the night's drinking, the taste of vomit only slightly tainting my evening and my breath.

I was also drinking throughout the day; a cider in the morning – hair of the dog, to start me off. Then slowly my drink of choice would get heavier: a gin and tonic with lunch, and then another before an afternoon nap. The drinking proper would start before I went out, though; shot after shot of sickly vodka schnapps, a bottle of wine . . . As the term went on, this drinking ritual became private. No longer did I grace my flat's kitchen with my presence. There was drinking to be done, and it had to be done quickly and efficiently. I started nailing straight spirits instead of schnapps – two fingers of vodka mixed with lemonade became three or four fingers, downed from an unclean glass. Drinking wasn't about fun any more. It was about being drunk. The effort of maintaining this happy, carefree personality was starting to take its toll, and the only time I felt comfortable was when I was drunk. Deep down, I hated the entire rigmarole: getting dressed up, talking to new people. What was it for? It was empty, and so was I. The good parts of my personality had vanished along with my crusty DMs.

I imagine I was hard to live with during this period. My behaviour was unquestionably weird and got weirder as term went on: never leaving my room, only using the kitchen at 3am, posting weird photos of myself on Facebook at 4am. I was probably a nightmare. But living with my flatmates was a nightmare for me too; constantly judging me, they finally dealt with my mental health problems by telling me that they didn't want to live with me, after all. I don't blame them, really; who, at nineteen, knows how to deal with that level of mania?

By the time I went back after Christmas, my mania was in full swing. It was the first real manic episode I had ever had, and I had no idea what was happening. I felt compelled to go to lectures and make notes, but when I read them back none of them seemed to make sense. I would send literally hundreds and hundreds of tweets a day, talking nonsense to celebrities and civilians alike, documenting my days in excruciating detail. I would log when my leg felt itchy or when I had a slight headache or if someone walked into the courtyard of my building. Every song I listened to was tweeted too, and my feelings on my flatmates, my course, myself and my boyfriend were all broadcast to an increasingly large, and probably horrified, audience. I didn't think to censor my thoughts because it felt so absolutely vital to record them. It was compulsive. People still ask me how I've managed to write 50,000 tweets – here's your answer.

My psychotic episode didn't *feel* like anything when it happened; it just felt normal. Now I'm older, I can sense when I'm likely to become delusional and swiftly text my best friend saying, 'I don't feel well'. And I often don't. I feel out of sorts before a psychotic episode comes on – slightly disturbed in a way I have tried and failed many times to describe. Something just feels off. But I simply didn't have that level of insight the first time it happened; didn't have the vocabulary to explain exactly how unsettled I felt.

Buoyed by mania, my behaviour had become ever more erratic. Then, as I feel I have typed a million times, came the inevitable crash. I was suicidal. I started self-harming in earnest again, brazenly displaying the scars to every horrified onlooker I could find, as if a reaction or an acknowledgement would validate the pain I was feeling and thus mitigate it somehow.

At my most desperate, I cut my arms from my wrist to my shoulder and went to get help from a housemate. Nobody was in, and I just slid down the corridor wall, utterly trapped by my own misery. When someone finally returned home and saw me there, covered in blood and clearly in distress, she simply stepped over my prone body and retreated to her own room. She locked the door.

Empathy can't – or shouldn't – be limitless; there's a point at which you really should stop making excuses for other people's shitty actions. And despite my particularly bad habit of reaching that point far, far too late, this was too awful for even me to excuse. I understand I was probably difficult to live with; I understand that watching someone go from fun, outgoing friend to psychotic hermit was probably confusing, difficult and not a little scary. Being confronted with something like that, especially for the first time in your life, can be truly terrifying. It's why people often say the wrong thing, why they don't understand that you can't just 'pull yourself together' or why they chummily tell you to cheer up. It's a spectrum, of course. At one end is someone who totally gets it, who always uses the correct terminology and offers you the absolute perfect support. Hardly anybody is there – not even me, most of the time. And at the other end is my housemate.

I don't know what advice I could give someone else in the situation I was in back then. 'Take care when choosing house-mates' might work later on in life, but it's pointless when it comes to university because happy first-year living is so dependent on the luck of the draw. Saying 'Ignore it' is all well and good, but it was too hurtful to ignore, too horrible to repress. It's stuck with me for five years, popping into my head at bizarre and unrelated moments – at night, when I'm drifting off to sleep, but also on the bus or at work and once, improbably, during sex. Lots of traumas – condensed down to anecdote, folded away neatly to fit a narrative – lose their edge. This hasn't. I still cannot believe that it happened. It still seems bizarre and preposterous and ridiculous to me. And it still seems like some kind of weird metaphor that would be considered far too broad in fiction. Surely she can't have just *stepped over me*? Surely it can't have happened the way I recall? But it did.

She may not even remember it. I doubt the incident is seared into her psyche as deeply as it is mine. What I hope is that if she does remember it, or in the unlikely event that she reads this book and it jogs her memory, she'd be ashamed of herself. To call an ambulance, another friend or just to sit down next to me and say, 'Are you OK?' would have required very little effort. Asking if I was all right might seem meaningless, but it would have been *something*. It would have been a gesture, a token nod towards the fact that I absolutely was not OK and that I needed to do something about it. To do nothing was – and is – fairly unforgivable in my eyes.

There's no way to say what it was about university that made me lose my mind so utterly. Alcohol didn't help, especially as it was my first real experience of it and my tolerance, now worryingly high, was close to zero. Sleeping all day and staying up all night was definitely a factor, and the stress of lectures, exams and socialising – the triumvirate of a successful university experience – weighed heavily on me.

Mainly, though, it was just being on my own and not knowing what to do or think. I had somewhat successfully distracted myself at school; there were always lessons I had to go to, homework to be done, exams to revise for. University gave me this huge expanse of unscheduled time in which I was meant to be productive, to achieve the things for which I had the capacity and potential. But unscheduled time means you have to be in your own company; you have to live inside your own head for hours or days at a time. It wasn't that I didn't know how to live alone, or live with others – it was that I didn't know how to live with myself.

* * *

So having seen how easily it can go wrong, how do you make it go right? Or, at least, how do you make it go less wrong than I did?

● **Remember you don't have to drink**

A table full of playing cards and empty bottles and nervous, giddy young people secretly desperate to impress each other is one of the most enduring images of Freshers' week. Drinking games are par for the course at university; there are lots of them, all designed to get you as drunk as possible as quickly as possible, and occasionally to humiliate you in front of new people while you're at it. I'm sure they have their appeal, although I've never quite seen it.

The point is, alcohol can have a serious effect on mental health. It can exacerbate depression or heighten feelings of mania; hangovers can induce anxiety attacks that feel like someone is physically squeezing your heart over and over again while you endlessly mentally replay whatever dumb thing you may have said the night before. If you know alcohol has this kind of effect on you and your mental health, or if you're worried about what a whole week of poor sleep, bad diet and excessive alcohol will do for you, then *do not feel that you have to drink.*

There are lots of reasons why someone might not drink, and plenty of fake excuses if you (understandably) don't want to share your mental health worries with your new flatmates. You could tell them you're on antibiotics and have to be careful what you drink, or that you have a really important job interview in the morning. Tell people you don't feel very well, or surreptitiously make your alcohol/mixer ratio incrementally smaller as the night goes on. If you're at the bar, just get a Coke or a lemonade – how will anyone else know whether or not it has vodka or gin in it?

You could also earmark certain days of the week for sobriety. Drinking at uni is less of a lifestyle choice and more of a necessity – as if some kind of unspoken decree has ruled that you must exceed ten units of alcohol a day. It's therefore not just nights-out that get you; it's that 'one drink' on a quiet night; it's the post-lecture pint or the pre-drinks you go to even if you're not going out. Try to cut back on this kind of casual non-drinking drinking. You never really *think* of this as drinking because why would you? 'Drinking' is going on the lash, 'drinking' is downing sickly fluorescent cocktails until you pass out. But drinking here and there adds up too – so if you can't avoid nights out, then cut down here. Have a pint of diet Coke instead of a pint of beer after your lecture; drink one beer instead of four when you're alone in your room watching Netflix.

Keep in touch with friends and family

It's always a good feeling when you turn up to halls on your first day of university and your flatmates don't appear to be completely intimidating. They seem nice. Not likely to murder you as you sleep! And you're probably not even going to be that annoyed when they 'borrow' food from your cupboard. This is amazing! It *can* be easy to form close bonds with your new flatmates and coursemates from the start, and many people go on to form lifelong friendships with people they meet at university. It can be difficult to predict which of these brand-new best friends is going to stick, though – those friendships may not even emerge until you're in your last year. And while you may have lots of friends to begin with, they are often shallow and based more on convenience and insecurity than any genuine connection. So talking about your mental health with these people is not always an option.

You may also feel that your mental health is something to be ashamed of – something that could put off potential friends. It's not, obviously. We all know that really. But I found that feeling hard to shake when I went to university, and so I never talked about it. And, as we have seen, that did not end up well for me.

So keep in touch with your existing friends and family, no matter how busy you are or how bowled over by new 'friends' and experiences. Communicate how you feel to them, tell them about the tiny embarrassments and the big fuck-ups and the ebb and flow of your moods. Schedule regular calls. This way you can tell them what's going on with you and you'll have something to look forward to.

Things like Skype, Facebook Chat and WhatsApp make it easier than ever to keep in touch with your friends and family; they know you *so well*, and realising that you have that support network, no matter how far away, can really, really help.

- **Remember university is not a homogenous experience**

Your friends may have gone to university and loved it; maybe your older siblings thrived. Perhaps they joined teams and went drinking; they lived with their first-year housemates for the remainder of their degree – friends they still see now. But that doesn't mean you will have, or should have, the same experience.

Mentally ill or not, everybody has a different experience of university. We're sold this glitzy idea of it as this super-fun place where everybody has a brilliant time, but that's just not the case for lots of people. Lots of people fucking *hate it*.

It may feel like you're missing out if you're not out drinking every night, but you're not. Find the things you enjoy and do them. Who cares what everybody else is doing? Joyfully and carelessly being yourself is one of the purest forms of pleasure you can have in life; start early.

How to live alone for the first time

Perhaps the worst part of going to university for me was living alone for the first time. As with many university-related things, the very real challenge of living alone is couched in jokes. Quips like 'Students have no idea how to boil a pan of water!' and, 'Taking your laundry home to your mum, eh?' may seem like playful riffs on filthy student life, but were actually very pertinent to how poorly I would cope alone.

I wasn't particularly spoiled as a child; I come from a comfortable background, but was expected to do chores and had a regular job before I left home. I cooked a bit – not every night, but I had a few dishes I could knock up quickly and proficiently that my mum and I would share. My room was fairly tidy too. It wasn't minimalistic by any stretch of the imagination, but compared to friends' rooms, which were often carpeted with dirty plates and clothes, I was pretty neat. I was not a student cliché; in fact, I'd go so far as to say I was vaguely self-sufficient.

So what followed when I went to university was probably fairly surprising. It actually started off OK. I would cook the same three-ingredient dish at least three times a week (pasta, tuna, cheese), but at least I was actually cooking. I did my washing up – a bit shoddily, maybe, but I did it. And I kept my room relatively tidy, my clothes clean, my bedding fresh.

Then depression hit.

As you've already seen from the self-care chapter, my ability to remain on top of day-to-day chores when depressed is lacking. If I'm depressed, I can do nothing. And so it was at university. The plates piled up. My bedding remained unchanged. My wardrobe became a pit of dirty laundry and muddy shoes. Going to the laundry room (which was housed in a small building at least three minutes away from my room) was impossible. In the end, I got washing powder and a kettle and washed my clothes by hand in the sink as and when I needed them. And instead of tumble-drying them, as my saner housemates would do, I then hung them up on the back of my door and dried them with a hairdryer. This *seemed* incredibly resourceful.

It *seemed* like the best idea anyone had EVER HAD. It wasn't. It really, really was not.

The worse this weird mess got, the harder it was to make a dent in the tidying and the more incapable I became of doing anything about it. So here are a few tips on how to successfully live alone, and how to deal with things if they get too much.

● Practise before you leave home

There are certain things you can prepare for in advance; cooking, for one. Learn to make a few staple meals – things like curries, stir fries, omelettes and pasta dishes. Not only are these dishes cheap, but you can make them healthily and (maybe most importantly) with minimal washing up. Try to get into a routine of tidying, cleaning and cooking for yourself before you leave. Which leads us to . . .

● . . . make – and stick to – tiny household goals

If you're anything like me, you'll let everything pile up until it's a huge unmanageable mess. If you can, try to make sure this doesn't happen. Before you get depressed, or before you realise you're overwhelmed and can't cope, put small and manageable systems into place. Make tidying a habit, and be strict with yourself. Make your bed every day. Put bleach down the toilet every other day. Get a laundry basket and put dirty clothes in it at the end of every day, instead of on the floor. A study from University College London found that it takes about sixty-six days to form a habit – which, in the long run, is nothing.

It may be tedious as hell, it may be boring and a little

bit tiring and kind of annoying. But it is so, so much easier than dealing with a huge pile of washing up and a gross, crusty toilet and a messy bed all at once.

Think of practical solutions to major problems

There is no avoiding things piling up sometimes; no matter how hard you try, if you're severely depressed you're going to be less able to cope. And that's *totally fine*. But if you have a series of practical solutions to the biggest obstructions, they can be a lot easier to deal with.

If you have a problem washing up after eating, use paper plates. Use tin foil instead of having to wash a baking tray every time you cook. Buy ready meals if you have to; lots of supermarkets have relatively healthy and cheap microwave meals now, and you can buy vegetables that steam in the bag in the microwave too. There will be a practical life-hack solution to anything you have a problem with. Just try to plan ahead, and think of them before you need them.

Stock up

Before you go to university, or when you first arrive, stock up on the practical things you may need. I often found that inspiration to finally clean and sort my life out came at 3am, but if I didn't have the things I needed, I'd go to bed again and not have another spike of energy for weeks.

There are lots of websites with long lists of 'student essentials' – have a look and see if you can stock up on things. You're probably not going to need a pizza cutter or an egg poacher when you're depressed, but a small supply of things like bleach, sponges and ready meals for when you start getting low can be really useful.

- **Try to stay in control of your finances**

This is a biggie. I got into a lot – *a lot* – of debt when I was at uni the first time, and it took me years to pay it off. This kind of thing can spiral out of control when you're depressed or manic because buying stuff either seems like something that might cheer you up a bit or, at manic worst, it will be a compulsion.

This is the most boring advice of all, but may be the most important. Make a weekly budget – how much you want to spend on food, alcohol, transport, clothes, whatever – and stick to it where you can, but at the very least, track it. This can make a big difference when it comes to holding on to your money.

Passing your exams

When Nietzsche said 'time itself is a circle', I'm fairly sure that he was referring not to the idea that the universe is an ouroboros of time and experience and expression, but to the inevitability of exams. From the age of ten to twenty-two exams loom large over every spring and summer, a perpetual presence that manages to taint almost every moment of pure joy. Having fun with your friends? Bad luck, you have to take your GCSEs in six months. At a party? Too bad – A Levels coming up. Christmas Day is all well and good, but shouldn't you be revising? And just got out of your final exam? Relief flooding your body like a burst dam full of hopes and dreams and new horizons? Yeah, fine, but you'll be getting your results soon, so you'd better nip that one in the bud.

Nobody likes exams, but as with all things, mental illness makes this dislike a lot more pressing and urgent. If I'm depressed, then there's no chance I'll do well because I'll be too listless and miserable and lethargic to bother revising; if I'm manic, I'll become astonishingly blasé about their importance, and grossly underestimate my own lack of knowledge. As such, my exam success has fluctuated dramatically, and largely been down to luck. I happened to be depressed during my GCSEs and subsequently underperformed by quite a staggering degree, but during my medicated sixth-form years I was in a far better state of mind and was able to absolutely nail my exams. My various stints at university followed the same pattern. In my first year, on the cusp of a psychotic episode, I didn't revise at all and instead went into my Philosophy of Science exam completely unprepared, eventually writing eight pages about Woody Allen, whose films I had never actually watched. I did not pass the exam. Later, on my final attempt at actually getting a degree, I managed to scrape by – but only just. It's a source of constant frustration; I like to think I'm intelligent, and I'm certainly engaged and interested in learning, but my mental health problems have always got in the way of me demonstrating that in any tangible way. As I have said, I wish I had received some support or guidance in terms of learning, especially during exams season.

I don't want to suggest that exams mean nothing – I never did particularly well in mine, and my life has turned out fairly all right – but my solitary example will not make you feel any less anxious about underperforming. Whether it's GCSEs, A Levels or final-year university exams, you rightly want to do well and tales of my own failure will do absolutely nothing to temper that desire. So, instead, here are some tips to help you get through your exams.

- **Maintain some perspective**

  Yeah, yeah, I know I just said that I wasn't going to tell you exams are meaningless, but it's my book and I'll contradict myself if I want to. Obviously, exams mean *something*. They mean the key to a certain university or a particular job or maybe your family put you under a lot of pressure to succeed. And that's fine; in fact, it's important. If they didn't mean anything, then why would you bother at all? Meaning something doesn't make them *everything*, though. Failing an exam, or not quite hitting the grade that you wanted, feels shitty. Oh man, does it feel shitty. But you can, and you will, pick yourself up afterwards and carry on. Maybe you'll adjust your plans, or maybe you'll retake the exam. Maybe you'll realise that what you wanted to do is not what you are actually suited to do. But what you will definitely do is survive. You will get to where you want to be. You will be OK.

- **Prepare far, far in advance**

  There are always those guys who say, 'I started revising like, three months ago? But no, I totally don't know anything at all, I'm definitely going to fail.' They always hog the library books. And they've always been revising for longer than everyone else. Ignore that guy. But also, maybe, take a few cues from that guy.

  If you know you're likely to be struck by a period of

poor mental health, prepare yourself well in advance. Make flash cards or notes before you really need to. Organise your files while you still can. Record yourself reading out said notes, so you can listen to them when you're too low to concentrate on reading. These are tiny things that can seem time-consuming and pointless in advance, but are invaluable when you're not coping.

Similarly, preparing can help with close-to-exam anxiety. Universities are often huge and hard to navigate, so find out what room your exam is in and visit it beforehand. Anxiety often focuses on small things like 'Will I get there on time?' rather than the larger, more tangible worries such as actually passing the exam, so knowing exactly where you're going and how long it will take to get there can alleviate some of this extra worry. Likewise, make sure you're prepared with the physical things you need for an exam way before exam season starts: calculators, pencils and pens or whatever. Buy them. Keep them somewhere safe. Don't leave it until the last minute.

• Communicate your need for help

As already discussed, asking for help can be hard. Knowing what to say, when to say it and what to ask for – it's all very difficult. But communicating that you need help now or in the future is incredibly important. Tell teachers or lecturers that you're struggling with mental illness. Tell your doctor that you're about to take exams.

Many schools and universities take this kind of thing into consideration – universities especially, as they can be far more flexible with when exams are sat. Pastoral support may not be appropriate or adequate (many institutions fail to provide adequate care), but it may provide you with a little respite or make you feel less panicked about the prospect of sitting your exams.

You may also be able to get counselling through your university health service, and many universities have 'nightlines' – phone services you can call when you're feeling depressed or under pressure. Everyone operating these services will be well trained regarding things like exams, and should be able to offer some genuine, practical advice or tangible help around exams season.

Contact your student-welfare team, which exist both university-wide and are specific to subjects and halls of residence – many have online resources, which can be invaluable, and you can contact them online too. You can also make appointments to see welfare staff, who may be able to point you in the right direction in terms of counselling, stress management, diet and more.

Resits are your friend

Once you get past GCSEs, resits are most definitely your friend. You can resit A Levels; you can resit university exams. You can even resit whole years or go back to college to take any level of exam again. Your first go is not your only chance for success. Think of it as a test run; it may take you a little longer than everyone else, but who cares? My mum always used to tell me that 'life isn't a race', which seemed like hopelessly misguided advice when everyone else was out there living their lives, but she was right; it took me far longer to complete my education than anyone else I know, but I'm now leading a much better life than I would have been had I continued living with unmanaged psychosis.

● **Prepare a roster of relaxation techniques**

Lots of people are sceptical when you mention these, but they do actually work. Exams can bring out unmitigated panic in even the calmest of people, whether they have clinical anxiety or not, so having a roster of relaxation techniques ready for when you're feeling particularly anxious can really help. There are breathing exercises, progressive muscle-relaxation methods and more at the back of the book (see pp. 215–16).

● **Take time out**

There is a tendency during exam period to feel as if every second not spent revising is a waste. This is not true.

Take regular breaks – hours if you need them, or days – to decompress and not think about revision. Break up your days with tiny acts of self-care: have a shower; walk down the road to buy yourself something nice to eat; splash some water on your face; take a day off and lie in bed, if you need to. Don't stretch yourself further than you have to because therein lies the start of a depressive episode, severe anxiety or maybe worse. Essentially: be kind to yourself.

These tips aren't the be all and end all (obviously, exam success also requires hard work and lots and lots of revision). And they're not glamorous either – 'make some flashcards' is probably not the insightful and revelatory mental health advice you were after. But they certainly help.

* * *

I eventually succeeded at university the third time round. I tried hard to stick to routines and stay on track and, while it was extraordinarily hard, I managed it. It wasn't quite the way I'd wanted; I had always imagined myself leaving university with First Class Honours, a tight-knit group of friends and a raft of exciting, fun and pleasant memories, none of which happened. But it didn't matter.

What I did manage to do was navigate depression and mania, recover from the worst psychotic episode of my life and still get a good degree. The classification wasn't (and still isn't) important, in either an existential or practical sense; I have never been asked about my degree since I graduated. But it represented a lot more to me. Not to get all mawkish about it, I've never been prouder than the day I sat my last exam. I had made it to the finish line, despite all else. It made no difference how I had got there, or how circuitous and arduous the journey was – I was in exactly the same place as everyone else.

I also realised how little it all mattered. I was pleased to have finished the course, obviously, but it was less because I now had a degree and more because I had proven something to myself. I had shown that despite everything – despite teenage depression and all the struggles I had experienced at university – my mental illness could never stop me from doing something I wanted to do.

CHAPTER 5

SELF-HARM AND SUICIDE

This chapter contains detailed discussion of self-harm and suicide. If you're likely to find this difficult reading, please do take a break or skip the chapter. Websites and numbers of charities that deal with these issues are at the back of the book (see p. 213); if appropriate, please utilise them.

Self-harm

There are lots of good quotes about drinking. Hemingway and Bukowski and Kerouac have all provided alcoholics across the world with elegant barbs about their drinking habits. Drugs too, have secured their place in the literary canon. In recent history, Burroughs and Huxley wrote paeans to the act of drug-taking, and in more distant memory so did Byron and Coleridge. Each of these writers has lent an air of glamorous gravitas to addictive behaviour, not only legitimising it, but also mythologising it, so that the act of drinking or taking drugs was elevated from mere hedonism to something transcendental. Whether it was the experience of being drunk or high that made the act meaningful, or the subsequent battle of will weaning themselves off their vice of choice, these men made addiction an art and art out of addiction.

Self-harm has not had any such literary sponsorship. Nowhere to be seen are the lyrical odes to self-mutilation; few people in literature, outside of Sylvia Plath, are associated with self-injury. The reason for this is twofold: one, the dominance of men in the literary canon; and two, the way we categorise the many forms of self-destructive behaviour.

For what started in my bedroom at thirteen, as I limply and impotently pressed a pair of blunt scissors into my arm, extended far into my adulthood into twenty-four-hour drug binges and sixty units a week and total, exhilarating emotional recklessness. Self-harm, by which I mean cutting or burning, is self-destruction writ large, after all. The only way it differs from drink or drugs is the physical mark it leaves on your body, the shameful evidence that you have a problem. It's less socially acceptable, but for many people it serves the same purpose: complete annihilation of the self.

Each vice is an elegantly designed shot, a vaccination against reality. When you're manic, drugs are an irresistible top-up to an already superb wave of raw, arrogant joy. Alcohol kneads the rawest edges of depression into something softer and more manageable. For me, though, the greatest love affair of all has been with self-harm.

It sounds romantic, and in a way it has been. My relationship with self-harm was its own self-sustaining ecosystem; secret out of necessity, my sole escape from the real world, it was almost like a real affair. Affairs are always found out, though; lies always unravel. And beyond the initial excitement, the rush of the forbidden, they're always unhealthy and destructive.

There are lots of theories about self-harm, lots of reasons why someone might do it. There's the old 'cry-for-help' theory, which dismissively posits that teenagers cut themselves purely for attention – as if feeling so desperately in need of attention that cutting themselves seems like the only option isn't a problem in and of itself.

Then there's the idea that it's the outward manifestation of an inner pain, an addiction to the endorphins released by a cut, a way of feeling something, no matter how painful, when you're otherwise numb. I'm still not sure what it was for me – why self-harm was so irresistibly enchanting. Some of it was the ritual: the glint of the blade, the rush of the pain, the release of it – the little fucked-up, masochistic thrill that accompanied every slash or burn or cut – the thick, hot blood, the scars that turned from red to purple to hard white lumps on the skin. Even as an adult, cutting has been a deeply primal, quasi-orgasmic physical release for me, so it must have felt utterly, mystifyingly thrilling when I was fifteen.

No person, relationship or event comes close to being as significant as my teenage self-harm was to me. It influenced everything. One of my first relationships, while just as mean-ingful and joyful and important as any other first love, was partly forged on a mutual appreciation for (or perhaps addic-tion to) physical pain. It was a secret we shared, a thing that set us apart in a vast sea of misunderstanding.

It was the same with one of my close friends at secondary school; our friendship was amazing and intense, but she too shared these masochistic tendencies with me. I'm sure every-body at school must have known: sleeves that remained resolutely rolled down, even on the hottest days, little glimpses of flushed skin or not-so-mysterious white scars . . . I was also behaving extremely oddly; as anyone with a secret can tell you, your ability to moderate your own behaviour gets somewhat lost among attempts to cover your tracks.

You might be thinking that 'addiction' is a rather grandiose phrase to associate with self-harm. It's not. Self-harm is often written off as attention seeking, as I've said, and even more frequently as a 'teenage girl thing'.* What that means, in broad cultural terms, is that it is facile. It is self-serving, maybe, and it is narcissistic. Teenage girls aren't given much respect generally, so anything that's even vaguely related to them is treated condescendingly and without much regard. I think this applies to all adolescents to some extent. Adults say that you can't possibly know yourself as a teenager; you can't experience anything real or sincere or profound. So what I and many other teenagers experience is written off.

So, what does count as an addiction? Broadly, according to the NHS, it's something you feel you have no control over and which has negative effects on your life. I haven't seen any better description for my own self-harm than this.

For years, it was a compulsion. It wasn't a choice in any real sense. When I tried to give up, I couldn't. I relapsed time and time again. Little marks on my calendar, counting cut-free days, turned straight back into little marks on my arms. I had help from parents, partners, friends, medical professionals; I blogged about it, tweeted about it, thought about it constantly. Still I couldn't give up. At my very worst, I was taking blades and razors to school with me every day, sneaking off to the

---

* The charity selfharmUK also suggests that it is more likely to affect girls than boys, although this may be because boys engage in behaviour that isn't classified as self-harm (such as punching walls). Nevertheless, the perception of self-harm tends to be gender stereotyped – in a negative way.

toilet during lessons and at lunch, getting a deep and illicit thrill from it.

I'm far from alone in my experiences; selfharmUK say that around 13 per cent of young people try to hurt themselves between the ages of eleven and sixteen, but it's hard to get a handle on the real figures. But the nature and stigmatisation of self-harm mean that many young people are unwilling to share details with friends or family, let alone statisticians. Countless friends have had similar experiences – some of whom I had discussed self-harm with in the past, and others who only mentioned it after I started writing this book. And there are thousands of young people across the country who have, or do, hurt themselves.

'It was a way of expressing how I felt on the inside,' said one friend who described self-harming as 'an absolute compulsion': 'I couldn't go a day without doing it,' she told me. 'It was all I thought about.'

Another friend – a man – told me that it gave him 'a sense of calm' that he just couldn't find anywhere else. He punched walls on a weekly basis (something that many people may not even consider to be self-harm), though his compulsion was identical to mine, and the results pretty similar too.

The reasons for self-harming I've heard from friends are disparate – an outer manifestation of inner pain, a distraction from trauma, a way to channel anger – but one thread running through all of them is clear: 'Nobody took me seriously.' With the exception of one friend, who had supportive family, friends and housemates, every person I've spoken to has come across somebody who questioned their behaviour or feelings. I heard it a lot too: 'Isn't self-harm just a phase? Don't you grow out of it?' Dealing with people who don't appreciate how desperate you feel, who think you're looking for attention, is just so tiring. Justifying yourself constantly, feeling as if you have to explain yourself – it's exhausting.

Then there's another section of the population: those who treat self-harm with unmitigated horror, which I've never quite understood. There are lots of ways pain and self-destruction can manifest themselves. Self-harm is just the most obvious. Drinking to excess three or four times a week, as friends of mine have done (and still do) is not healthy. Being dependent on drugs, or taking too many too often, is not healthy either. A compulsion to sleep around is not necessarily healthy; casual sex can be incredibly fun, but feeling like you *need* to have sex isn't good. What sets self-harm apart from all of these? The others can be purely recreational, yes, but when they reach these extremes it goes beyond fun, beyond recreation, and I find it puzzling that drink and drugs, which can be so damaging, aren't seen in the same way as physical harm of oneself.

I think the problem lies in the tangible physical results of self-harm. For many people, seeing scars or cuts or burns is viscerally uncomfortable. They force people to acknowledge the reality of your pain; someone who drinks a lot or sleeps around, especially a woman, can be categorised under the conveniently neat term 'mess'. 'Oh, she's a mess', people say, not taking into consideration exactly why somebody would behave like that. 'He's having a hard time at the moment which is why he's drinking loads'. It's all euphemistic, though, all couched; none of it serves to illustrate exactly how desperate a person can feel while they're careering from one bad hookup to another, one sticky-floored bar to the next. Self-harm is not euphemistic. It is blunt. Self-harm says, 'I am hurting'.

And that's an uncomfortable thing to hear, especially if you love someone.

It's a matter of relatability too; most people who drink or take drugs have gone too hard on occasion, or recognise the desire to do so. Lots of people have regretted a one-night stand. Self-harm, though, is an unknown quantity; it's out of most people's sphere of experience by quite some way. They can't relate to it, and that horrifies them.

Coping strategies

It took me a long time to give up self-harm. I still do it from time to time, when I'm feeling really desperate, but the urge just isn't there in the same way it used to be, and I've pretty much kicked the habit. There's no compulsion now, no sitting daydreaming about knives or blood while I'm on the bus.

It wasn't easy, though. It took time, patience and a lot of relapsing before I managed to wean myself off it. I had a daily battle with whether or not I even *wanted* to give up. It was my only emotional crutch, after all, and taking it away meant that I found it harder than ever to cope.

If you're thinking of giving up, there are a few things you can do to distract yourself. These are techniques that have helped me and various friends, both long- and short-term; they might not be a way of stopping completely, but they can help give you a brief respite from the compulsive urge to hurt yourself. The Royal College of Psychiatrists also advocates distracting yourself, so there is a chance this may help you out.

Coping techniques can be split into a few categories: *distracting* yourself, *comforting* yourself, *physical expression* and *introspection*.

• **Distracting yourself**

This is probably one of the easiest ways to delay or prevent yourself from self-harming. All you have to do is focus on something else (although, having said that, it can be easier said than done). You can do this by:

- ▶ watching a film
- ▶ reading a book
- ▶ doing a puzzle/jigsaw/crossword
- ▶ playing a videogame
- ▶ calling a friend.

Basically you can do anything that will briefly distract you, whatever it is that you're into. I often find that measuring the distraction out into strict time periods helps: 'I'm not going to cut myself for ten minutes,' for example. Small sections of time are easy to fill – one episode of a TV show is twenty minutes, at least – and you may find that the desire to hurt yourself has passed or, at the very least, lessened after ten minutes.

• **Comforting yourself**

This tends to fall under the self-care category, so try some of the techniques you learned there (see pp. 30–61). Comforting things can be grounding, so they're most likely to work when your desire to self-harm is frantic and you need to calm down. Some ideas:

- ▶ Have a bath.
- ▶ Have a nap – lots of blankets, lots of pillows, lovely soft PJs.

- ► Meditate or do some breathing exercises.
- ► Smell something nice – aromatherapy oils can help here.
- ► Put on some fresh pyjamas and watch some TV.

• Physical expression

This is a good way of releasing pent-up energy *and* distracting yourself. There are some pretty corny ways of doing this – you're probably going to feel dumb screaming into a pillow, for example – but no matter how ridiculous they seem, they can actually help. Ideas:

- ► Punch something (a pillow or a punchbag rather than a person, please).
- ► Squeeze ice between your fingers (this will also hurt because of the cold, so can provide some of the masochistic relief you're after without any of the more severe and lasting damage of cutting or burning).
- ► Squeeze a stress ball.
- ► Do some exercise – go for a run, walk or cycle.

• Introspection

This is less physically fulfilling than the rest of the suggestions here, but it can both provide a brief distraction and also help you figure out what it is you're feeling or what the self-harm you're craving is compensating for.

- ► Write down your feelings. This can be a way of expressing how you feel without hurting yourself, even if you delete it or throw it away afterwards.

► Talk to a friend about how you're feeling.
► Express yourself creatively – write a poem or a song or an article.

Staying safe and first aid

If you really want to self-harm, there is nothing I can say to you that will stop you from doing it. The techniques above are great, and I strongly encourage you to try them, but I'm two things: one, a realist; two, an ex self-harmer.

I know first-hand how impossible giving up can seem. I know the thrill you get from self-harming. I understand how great it sometimes feels in the moment of relapse. And if you absolutely have your heart set on hurting yourself, then I cannot talk you out of it. What I can do, however, is make sure you're doing it safely.

● **Make sure your self-harm apparatus is sterile**

This is probably most pertinent to cutters. In their Harm Minimisation guide selfharmUK encourage leaving blades in boiling water or sterilising fluids, and urge you to never share a blade.

● **Aftercare is important**

It may not seem it, but making sure that your cuts or burns are clean is extremely important. A very small cut I had once got infected and it was not only painful but disgusting. It seeped and oozed pus, and it made my whole arm ache for days.

If you burn yourself, then remove clothing from the

area, apply lukewarm water and cover with clingfilm. If you cut yourself, first try to control the bleeding by applying pressure to the wound. If it's a large cut or wound, press the edges together. Clean the wound and cover it with a sterile dressing.

Cleaning a wound is actually very easy, and you don't need any special equipment to do it – only things you can buy in any pharmacy and which you can easily store away somewhere discreet. Once the cut has stopped bleeding, clean it using regular tap water. Antiseptic might seem like a good idea, but the NHS don't recommend it, as it can damage the skin or make healing a lot slower. Once it's washed, dry the wound with a (clean!) towel and apply a dressing. This can be a plaster or a dressing pad, depending on what's available. Change this regularly and keep it dry, and after a few days the cut should be well on its way to healing. All of this advice is taken from the NHS Choices guide to caring for cuts and grazes, and has always served me well.

• Keep an eye out for infection

As I have said, infections are gross. They hurt, they're unsightly and, most of all, they're dangerous. If a wound looks excessively swollen or red, or is suddenly hurting more than usual, then it's a sign it may be infected. You may see pus coming out of the wound or feel generally ill. If you see any of these signs, please go to your doctor; it can easily be treated with antibiotics.

• **If you need it, get help**

If you injure yourself too badly, *go to A&E*. Do not leave a serious wound untended because you're nervous about what will happen if you go to hospital.

If blood is pumping out of the wound in time with your heartbeat, then chances are you've hit an artery – please call an ambulance or get to A&E as soon as you can. Chemical burns should always, always be seen by a doctor.

You can find out more information on self-harm-related injuries from the charity LifeSIGNS, and NHS Direct have loads of first-aid advice on their website.

* * *

Just because I don't self-harm as much these days doesn't mean I don't harm myself in other ways; drinking, drugs and other reckless behaviour should also be considered self-harm. These things happen far less frequently than before, though, and the compulsion is far less overpowering; when I find myself thinking about cutting myself, for example, I don't feel the keen and sharp need that bubbled and broiled in my chest until I alleviated it with a razor blade or scalpel. My ruminations are now much more logical: maybe if I cut myself, I might feel better, I think to myself very calmly. This means I do it much less often: if my emotions aren't strong enough, they can be fairly easily overcome by logic.

It's taken a combination of things for me to get to this point. I've been in therapy on and off for a long time, which has helped. I've talked about self-harm publicly – anonymously at first, on a blog, and then more openly as my career became writing for a living. Sharing stories with other people about self-harm and making sure that it wasn't a secret any more was incredibly freeing for me. Some of the allure of self-harming for me was the fact it was a clandestine thing, something I wasn't telling anyone about, so getting rid of that element allowed me to deal with it properly.

The most important thing for me, I think, was taking it day by day. It ties in with SMART goals (see p. 58), and with the taking-it-ten-minutes-by-ten-minutes technique (see p. 128). Feeling I had to stop, with no time frame or strategies in place, was impossible. But taking it day by day – and, within that day, hour by hour and minute by minute – I was able to slowly stop. A day is nothing; a day is easy. And slowly the days add up. Sometimes you have to start from zero again – and that's OK – but slowly, steadily, one minute becomes one hour becomes one day becomes one year.

Suicide

Suicide sits rather awkwardly in the cultural imagination. Like addiction, it's somewhat romanticised; it's tragic and unknowable, it robs us of writers and artists and musicians. But it's stigmatised too, denounced; it was a crime in the UK until 1961, and the subsequent social, religious and moral hang-ups associated with this legislation don't really seem to have dissipated yet.

Modern arguments against suicide may not take such an explicit stand against religious mores or 'crimes against the Crown', but their basis is much the same; suicide is immoral because it goes against the 'natural order of things'. The sense of self that many of us identify with resembles dualism more than anything else; most people unconsciously perceive their 'mind' to be distinct from their body. And suicide is an attack on both of these.

Unlike most other phenomena that fall under the vague umbrella of 'mental distress', suicide is not thought of sympathetically. Depression and bipolar and anxiety are all stigmatised and stereotyped and misunderstood, but there's a level of understanding that even the most pig-headed are able to grasp. Everybody has experienced sadness or despair, and depression is the logical conclusion of these things. Everybody's been nervous or worried about something, and if you explain to a sceptic that anxiety feels like that, but *all of the time*, they will broadly understand it. But like psychosis, suicide does not seem like the logical conclusion of anything. It seems counterintuitive, unreasonable. It seems unjustifiable.

It's weird, really, because to me suicide often seems entirely logical. It's what happens when you've had enough; it's what you contemplate when you're so backed into a corner that nothing else is an option. People don't just wake up one day and think, 'Oh, maybe I should kill myself' – it's not a decision that's made without deep and extended thought.

I don't think there's any unpicking the morality of suicide; much better and more intelligent writers have done that before me, so there's not much point. But what I can do is talk about my own experiences of being suicidal – maybe to humanise it a bit, or maybe to make you feel less like you're weak or selfish or attention-seeking for even acknowledging that you might want to kill yourself.

A brief history of wanting to die

The first time I really wanted to die I was fifteen. As eagle-eyed readers will probably already have gathered, I was pretty depressed. I don't really know where the idea that I might kill myself came from but once it materialised it lodged in my brain, where it has remained ever since.

At first my desire to kill myself filled me with anxiety; it made me antsy, nervous. I think I felt as if I might find myself half-dead before I realised what I was doing. But as I got used to it – the planning, the endless tossing and turning of ideas and concepts and pros and cons – it became soothing in a way. My actual suicide attempts – which have been shoddy, badly planned and ultimately (and obviously) unsuccessful – took me from the vague, conceptual realms of 'I wish I was dead' to a very real understanding that I could literally kill myself at any point. If I suddenly decided that life is ultimately a zero-sum game, that I'd achieved all I wanted to and there was nothing left in it for me, I could kill myself. This was quite calming.

Suicide is a curious kind of tunnel vision. When you're suicidal you think of nothing else; weeks lost to aimless daydreams that always end with you under the wheels of a bus or lying dead in scarlet bath water. It almost becomes banal; like the doodles you do in a boring lecture or a point-less meeting if they were all incredibly detailed and involved coffins and organs and blood.

I often come across as glib when I'm talking about suicide, and I think that can be unsettling for some people. It's not that I don't take it seriously; quite the opposite, in fact. But I casu-ally describe how I've planned so sincerely and comprehensively for my own death simply because discussing it in any other way is impossible for me. I just don't know how else to do it. I think this is because it's so surreal, so ridiculous, so counterintuitive, to wish yourself dead that I swing between calm logic – 'I was only doing what seemed to make the most sense at the time' – and absolute disbelief, and can find no way to reconcile the two.

I also don't know how in the midst of experiencing profound despair I was able to conjure up the kind of systematic organisational skills I lack even when I'm stable. Every step of each suicide attempt was calmly and efficiently carried out with military precision; normally, I can't even plan what I'm going to have for dinner each night of the week.

The despair of suicidality is much more visceral for me than the blank numbness of 'normal' depression. Depression is numb and grey and lifeless; being suicidal is like the darkest black of the deepest void. It feels like something is constantly crawling across your body – and I mean that literally, rather than figuratively. It's terror rising all the time without the climactic relief of a panic attack. It doesn't feel like 'giving up' because 'giving up' is passive; instead, it combines the nervous energy of mania with the misery of depression. It's like someone constantly goading you to *just do something*. But any time you try to do something – anything – you feel impotent. Getting drunk does nothing; neither does going out to see friends. Self-harm doesn't help, and neither does sex. Everything feels as if it's leading up to some bursting, some breakthrough – instead, the pressure intensifies more and more.

As I've said, though, it's also calm and sensible and reasonable. It's browsing the Internet to look up toxic doses of medications, comparing lists of drugs that have deadly inter-actions. It's waking up and planning your day in minuscule detail: get up, go to work, don't forget that leftover lasagne, go to three different pharmacies at lunch to stockpile pills, come home, die. It's thinking ludicrous things like, 'I can't kill myself tonight because yesterday was bin day and I don't want the rubbish to rot and stink the flat up, so I'll wait until next week,' – as if that's totally normal.

There's this idea that anyone who thinks about suicide is 'crazy' in the most pejorative sense, but for me it just doesn't feel like that. For me, it's like I'm making the most rational decision of all. And I think, at heart, that's what terrifies so many people. It's very easy to dismiss suicidal thoughts as somehow irrational, and in a way they are; we're genetically and biologically hardwired to survive, after all, and you could even go so far as to say that living long enough to reproduce is the only purpose we have at all. Resisting that biological destiny is madness in the truest sense; it's absurd and mind-less and pointless. To write off suicide as an expression of such senseless madness is the easiest explanation, because it says nothing profound or interesting about the mind, nothing worrying about the human existence. It demonstrates nothing but the human capacity for lunacy. It protects people from the worrying thought that such madness could touch them.

But most suicides aren't like that; neither are most people who think about, but never attempt, suicide. Of course, in many cases there's an element of 'madness'. Lots of people who attempt or think about suicide are severely mentally ill. But there's no getting away from the fact that at the heart of suicide is a deliberate and level-headed decision. A person's judgement may be clouded; they may not be able to understand that things will get better. But they're not swept away by hysteria. They're not delirious. They're just unhappy.

What to do if you feel suicidal

● **Talk to someone**

The most important thing to do when you feel suicidal is to *talk to someone*.

You may feel too depressed to organise it, but going to see a therapist or counsellor if you don't already can be a really good step to take when you're feeling suicidal. This also goes for visiting your GP, support worker or psychiatrist to get medication or a referral to another team. If you feel like you don't have the energy to call and make an appointment – or attend it – try to talk to a friend or person you trust who can help you take the practical steps you need to go and speak to a professional.

You can also call helplines: the Samaritans phone lines (which you can reach on 116 123 in the UK) are manned by extremely well-trained and empathetic people, or, if you're at university, there's your uni Nightline service.

There are also lots and lots of great online resources around suicidal thoughts. Again, Samaritans have a website if you don't want to call them, as do Mind, the Mental Health Foundation, CALM and more. Contact details for all of these charities are at the back of the book (see p. 213).

● **Try to keep yourself safe and away from triggers**

When I'm horribly depressed and prone to feeling suicidal, the thing I am most likely to consider is taking an overdose.

When I start feeling like this I remove all of the medication from my home as far as I can. Sometimes I'll get a friend to stay with me, who keeps hold of any medication I need and gives it to me daily.

If you can, try to do the equivalent. Remove sharp objects from your house, or hand them over to a friend. Mind uses the example of someone who drives dangerously when suicidal: if this is the case with you, give your car keys to someone you can trust.

It's not always easy to remove yourself from triggers or potential suicide methods, but these are small ways of protecting yourself from them until you feel safer.

• Distract yourself

Again, this is a short-term measure – it's really best to talk to a friend or professional about how you're feeling – but it can be a way of keeping yourself safe in the interim.

Try distracting yourself with the methods discussed in the self-harm section (see p. 128): have a relaxing bath, watch your favourite TV shows, go for a walk, paint your nails – basically anything to bide the time until you feel very marginally better.

• Prepare in advance

Prepare an emergency plan comprising all of the above for when you're feeling suicidal. Know in advance exactly who you'll want to contact and what you'll need to do, and have a box or drawer full of distraction techniques and self-care items at the ready.

Myths about suicide

If you put aside the grander notions of suicide as romantic tragedy, you find a number of even more troubling ideas. Peel back the layers of insincerity – 'Such a shame', 'What an awful tragedy' – and you'll find many people's true opinion on suicide: that it's selfish, for example, or that it's an attempt at attention seeking that's gone too far.

As mental health becomes a far more prominent topic, it seems odd that these myths should continue. Education remains vital here; when I spoke to a friend, Jonny, whose brother killed himself a few years ago, he told me that this could be the key to stopping the myths: 'I was taught about disease in biology, and physical fitness in PE, but we never discussed mental health to any degree.' He thinks we should teach children about mental health – he describes schoolkids as a 'captive audience' and thinks that the opportunity to 'teach them right there and then about depression, anxiety, suicide and mental health' is too good to pass up.

'In school you have the chance to let them know that it's not unusual to feel low, you have the perfect moment to try to end the stigma,' he says. 'Everybody just needs better, more widespread and more in-depth education on the matter of mental health, and to acknowledge that things aren't going to change overnight. It could take years, decades or even generations to change opinions and beliefs, but if in the end it saves lives and keeps people around it can only be a good thing.'

Lack of education really does lead to the perpetuation of these myths. Not only are they offensive, they're largely based on misunderstandings or flat-out mistruths. If you've missed the boat for a school-age education on suicide, here are a few brief debunkings.

- **Suicide is selfish**

The thing you hear the most about suicide is that it's selfish. 'She should have thought of her family' and things of that ilk are often thrown around in the aftermath of a suicide. It seems to suggest that suicidal people don't care about their friends or family, which couldn't be further from the truth. Wondering to yourself whether, or how, friends and family would cope with your death is a major part of suicidal rumination, and it's not a decision that's come to lightly. Nobody fails to consider these repercussions. Nobody.

In my opinion, a person can never be called selfish for asserting their own autonomy; if someone is in so much pain that continuing to live is too terrible, I think they're absolutely within their rights to make an informed decision about carrying on. The idea that they have been 'selfish' in committing suicide suggests that there were other options open to them besides one where they remained alive but continued to suffer, or one in which their suffering came to an end. That just isn't how it works. To consider suicide a person is at the absolute end of their tether; they can't possibly understand how they could carry on living.

All of that aside, I think the main problem with saying that suicide is selfish is that it just isn't helpful. The stigmatisation of suicide – and, by extension, suicidal feelings – is rife. Even now, with my extensive professional and personal experience talking about mental health, suicide is a taboo that causes the most awkward winces or strained silences.

'Nobody told me to my face that my brother was being selfish, but it's certainly a feeling that's out there,' Jonny told me. 'You see a lot of memes that get shared on Facebook and Twitter about how we should treat mental health the same way we treat physical health, with a picture of a guy with a broken leg being told to quit crying about it or what have you. But there seems to come a point where people stop wanting to treat mental health the way they treat physical health, and that point is where suicide is involved.'

He talks about how somebody could battle cancer for years, attend chemotherapy sessions, take their medication, but eventually pass away. 'Similarly, someone can battle depression for years, go to therapy sessions, take their medication, but ultimately lose the battle too. In only one of those circumstances would the person who died be called "selfish". It's a flippant comparison I'll admit, but if people want to treat mental health as they do physical health it needs to be followed through to its logical conclusion.'

Demonising people who have killed themselves is horrible for them, for their families and for those who also feel like they might want to die. Your mum was right: if you have nothing nice to say, don't say anything at all.

- **People who are genuinely suicidal would never talk about it**

This one is not so much of a value judgement as the rest, and it *kiiiind* of makes sense. If you were serious, you wouldn't tell anyone your plans because that might prevent you from carrying them out, right?

Wrong.

In actual fact, research has found that many people who kill themselves have discussed their feelings or plans with others beforehand. Samaritans also make the point that it's incredibly important to take anybody seriously if they say they're suicidal. If someone confides in you about feeling suicidal, then don't think, Meh, they won't do it. Think, How can I get this person the help that they need? How can I help them access the services that they might require? How can I listen to and respond to their needs?

• Suicide is attention seeking

I kind of covered this under self-harm, but the same applies here too. A very small percentage of people may use self-harm or suicide to 'seek attention', but what's wrong with that? If someone has no way of expressing a desire for help or regard other than through harming themselves, then what they need *is* help.

In a stable state of mind, I would never *dream* of acting as if I wanted to kill myself for 'attention', and that goes for the vast majority of people who express suicidal thoughts. If they're asking for attention, give it to them.

• Suicide is weak

The idea that people who are mentally ill are 'weak' is something that really bothers me. What does it even *mean*? That they can't cope? That they fail to complete tasks that 'normal' people do? That they find things stressful? That they're deficient in some way? Weakness is something that comes up with mental illness in general and suicide in particular and it is *such bullshit*.

Waking up every day and feeling depressed is hard. Making your way through your working day as you go through psychological and physiological strain is hard. Dealing with traumatic experiences is hard. Ruining relationships and putting yourself at risk because you're manic is hard. Navigating the world when you're constantly anxious is hard. And you know what? Most people get through it. Most people work through their problems and reach a stage where they're living a fairly stable life alongside their mental health problems. They might relapse, sure, but people keep going. People have jobs and relationships and lives, even though they might be in intense distress. Does actually feeling this distress make them weak? Because to me it looks a lot like strength.

To suggest that someone is somehow weak because they decide that no, they can't deal with the immense pressure they're under is abhorrent to me. It's judgemental. It says, 'Well, *I* could probably get through it'. And it supports the narrative that people with mental health problems are somehow not *trying* hard enough; if they just *tried* to be strong, they'd be able to get through it. Well, that just isn't the case.

When I've been at my most suicidal, the idea that I have some kind of moral deficit – that because I can't cope I'm broken and weak and too feeble to survive in an unforgiving world – has made me feel worse. It has made me want to die all the more. If I'm so inexorably weak, then what's the point. If I can't summon the 'strength' to fight what feels like an unending battle, then my logic is right, after all: I should be dead.

How to support a suicidal friend

So: myths busted, stigma ignored, what do you do next? What do you do if someone you love has expressed suicidal thoughts or you're worried about their behaviour? As with all things, every situation is unique and context dependent, but there are a few things to remember.

- **Withhold any and all value judgements**

  Most people are pretty good at this, but I have had quite a few experiences of confiding in people who've responded to tearful, genuine pleas for help with 'Don't be so stupid'. I mean, maybe killing myself *would* be stupid, I don't know. But does actually telling me that help? No. It does not. So even if you do have a less than sympathetic view of suicide, please keep it to yourself.

- **Don't 'bargain' with them**

  This is another one of those 'I'm-sure-you-probably-mean-well-but-god-you're-really-not-helping' things. Yes, I know I have plenty to live for. Yes, I know people love me. Yes, I understand in the vaguest and most hypothetical sense that things can – and maybe will – get better. Telling me this doesn't actually help, though. Trying to bargain with me – 'I'd miss you too much if you kill yourself' – doesn't help. I understand that's true, and well-meaning, and kind, but it just doesn't help. It makes me feel guiltier for one, and it makes me feel like even more of a fuck-up. How can I want to die with all of these people rooting for me? Why are they not enough for me? How did I become so self-absorbed? So selfish?

Better, for me, is someone simply listening to me and acknowledging that my pain and my desire to die are valid. I'm not saying they should tell me I'm *right*, as such – 'yeah fair enough, knock yourself out' – but more it's important that they appreciate that how I'm feeling is OK.

Worse still, in all seriousness, is saying, 'If you kill yourself, I'll kill myself.' There is no need for me to explain why this does not help.

• Talk to them

Mind, Samaritans and pretty much every chapter in this book offer the same advice: talk to them!

Let's face it: talking about suicide is really difficult. But here are a few things you can try: ask open-ended questions which allow them to discuss as little or as much as they want; ask them how they're feeling about suicide to try to ascertain what their plans or feelings are; and listen to what they have to say. Always, if in doubt: listen.

• Encourage them to get help

Suicidal people are often resistant to seeking or receiving help, but it's still worthwhile encouraging this. If they're worried about making appointments with doctors or psychiatrists, call the surgery for them or take them to their appointments. Help them find help resources online. Even if these resources aren't particularly relevant, the fact you've made the effort can often mean a lot.

During my last period of being suicidal, I had two particular friends who helped me out and urged me to go to the doctor. They also took me to the pub once a week, we would have lunch all the time, they listened to me say the same things for weeks on end and they were patient and kind when I was rude or when I ignored their messages. All this was hugely helpful; the fact that they encouraged me to get help was a bonus.

* * *

I can't say my oscillating desire to die has dimmed much over the years. From my first dabble with death at fifteen to more recent trips to the psych ward, it's something I've dealt with for a while and can't particularly see abating.

I'm loath to wholeheartedly subscribe to the 'It-always-gets-better' narrative because I think this betrays a fundamental misunderstanding of how mental illness works, but so far I've managed more than eighteen months without trying – or really wanting – to kill myself, and I can't even begin to envisage myself wanting to die as much as I have done in the past. It seems faintly ridiculous to say that I'm 'proud of myself' for simply being alive, but when wanting to die is the norm, each day I'm still here is an achievement in itself.

If you need help dealing with suicidal thoughts, please check the back of the book (pp. 213–17) for a list of helplines and resources designed to help you.

CHAPTER 6

FAMILY AND FRIENDS

Family

Families are complex and delicate ecosystems. The smallest thing can cause them to temporarily lose their balance; larger disruptions can change their structure and atmosphere for ever. Each of them is unique and impenetrable, too, and navigating them can be an alchemic combination of experience, guesswork and luck.

So what happens when this ecosystem is distorted by mental illness? How do families change when one of their party becomes depressed, or too anxious to cope? And how do you even communicate what you need from them?

The answer, rather unsurprisingly, depends on the family.

We all know how hard living with mental illness is (you're six chapters in, so if you're still on the fence, I'm not sure I can help you), but what's often ignored is how it affects those around you. Of course, we all know people who make their partner, friend or family member's mental health problem all about them, but in a more general sense there's very little discourse around carers or co-habitants.

I've had mixed experiences in this area. My family are great, but it's not always been easy – particularly for my mum, who I've lived more or less alone with throughout my childhood, adolescence and (unluckily for her) adulthood to date.

The intersection between family life and mental illness is probably most evident during adolescence. Most people still live with their families when they're teenagers, and it's a time when mental illness often starts to develop. This makes things even harder: you're unsure of yourself to begin with, you're dealing with mental health problems for the first time, *and* you have to get along with your family while doing so. This often makes for a rather unhappy combination.

I know my parents wouldn't disagree with me if I said they initially dealt with my mental health problems relatively poorly. They've always, always *tried* to help, they've always tried to understand, they've nearly always acted in a way they felt was most appropriate. That doesn't mean they always got it right, though. My mum, confronted with my probably rather alarming self-harm habit, told me I was being 'silly'; attempts to bribe me out of it with treats unsurprisingly failed; and secret scars that were inevitably discovered were often met with anger, exasperation and disappointment. Her reaction was altogether rational, though: of course she was angry, of course she was upset, of course she was exasperated. But none of this went very far in terms of assuaging my guilt or undoing my destructive urges.

I felt as if she didn't understand because she just wasn't *trying* enough; explaining the reasoning behind self-harm to yourself is hard enough, let alone trying to articulate it to your own mother. My argument that it was just the same as drinking a lot didn't go down well; drinking was normal to her and so, to an extent, were drugs. The fact I would willingly cut myself was so far outside of her experience that she had no real frame of reference in which to let my secret habit quietly sit. She dealt with it the only way she could; which is to say, she had no idea what she was doing. And I don't blame her.

We also fought a lot when I moved back in after dropping out of university. I had become used to exercising my own autonomy, and although that mainly consisted of sleeping in late and eating party rings at 11 o'clock at night, I resented having those spurious freedoms taken away from me.

I was also very depressed. Having dropped out in a spectacularly ridiculous fashion, I had very few friends left from university, and I was forced to sit alone in my rural childhood home, literally and figuratively miles away from the people whose happy university experiences were documented in minute detail on Facebook feeds I bitterly obsessed over.

These factors conspired to make me even more miserable, as well as bitter and crabby and spiteful; basically, every synonym you can think of for 'bad-tempered'. I rejected any attempt at affection because accepting it would require me to let my guard down, which was something I couldn't manage. My experience with psychosis had hardened me, and my subsequent depression wasn't doing much to soften my now completely glassy heart. As a result, I spent most of my time making barbed and, in hindsight, not particularly funny remarks about my family, what was on TV, people I saw on the street, a child who lived across the road who I had decided I hated and, most of all, my own mother. I was a nightmare: a terrible, half-formed monster who had outgrown adolescence, but failed to develop the critical faculties of adulthood. We fought in increasingly bitter ways.

When I asked my mum how she'd found that period, she said it was 'one of the most difficult years of her life'. Some of the words she used to describe me at that time included 'impatient', 'irrational', 'bad-tempered' and 'prone to complete meltdowns'.

My mum's approach to dealing with a problem is by talking about it endlessly – a habit partners will unhappily confirm that I've inherited. But her desire to talk goes far further than mine. She thinks that talking is the secret key to everything. And as someone who was deeply depressed, this approach irritated me. My mum, in her own words, 'begged' me to go to the doctor's, and while she still thinks my reluctance to do so was irrational, to me it was understandable. I had been forced to drop out of university; I had no friends. I was thinking about applying to do another course but a year felt like an impossibly long time, and there was no guarantee I would get in. What was there to talk about? More to the point, considering my circumstances: who *wouldn't* be depressed?

She was also keen that I go back to therapy, which I resented too. The days on which we drove to the doctor's office in palpably strained silence were the worst of all; I didn't want to talk, I just wanted to lie on the sofa and tweet inanities at strangers.

In the end, the therapy started to work. My job at a supermarket, though menial, gave me a new set of friends and a vague sense of purpose and I slowly pulled myself out of depression. I was a lot easier to deal with then, I imagine, and was certainly a lot less acerbic. Still, the situation taught me a lot about living with someone who didn't really know how to deal with my mental health problems – and even more about how to talk to family about them.

It's hard to talk about mental health with family members. It's really hard. I don't know why, exactly; your family are the closest thing to you in both a literal and figurative sense. And while it's certainly not true in all cases, I think it's fair to say that most parents will love their children unconditionally, and especially if they have mental health problems, which are never anybody's fault. There's a tension, though, between remaining under the familial wing and being your own person; in asserting your bodily and psychological autonomy, yet wanting reassurance and protection. It's a taut, tough tightrope to walk.

It can also be hard when more than one member of the family has a mental illness. My mum is incredibly anxious, and has had experience of severe anxiety disorders, agoraphobia and OCD. If she's feeling particularly anxious, it manifests itself in obsessive checking – checking light switches are off, unplugging electrical equipment, checking a very specific number of times whether or not the oven and hob are turned off. If I'm feeling stable, it's fine – I'll tell her she needs to get support, try to help her out, do the best I can. If I'm depressed, however, it can get ugly.

Perhaps unsurprisingly, when we lived together the depression/anxiety combination didn't really work for us. I was depressed; she became anxious about my depression. Her anxiety felt stifling to me; I pushed her further away, became more introverted, made her more anxious. Her anxiety irritated me; without the empathy I would normally have mustered, it just seemed overbearing. We argued a lot; nothing was ever resolved. Only later, with the help of medication and hindsight, did I see what a difficult cycle we'd managed to get ourselves into.

My dad has depression, but as we've never lived together for any significant amount of time, there hasn't been a particularly explosive interaction. His experiences of mental illness and parenthood haven't been as easy, though. His mum had many symptoms of what would now be diagnosed as bipolar. She was addicted, at various points, to prescription pills, cough medicine and alcohol. This was back in the days when cough medicine had all sorts in it – morphine and cocaine extract and other stuff you probably wouldn't get in a bottle of Calpol. She would send my dad, aged eight or nine, to chemists and doctors' surgeries across their small Welsh town, equipping him with excuses he'd recite in his head in the waiting room so as not to get them wrong: she'd lost her pills, put them in the wash by accident, lent them to a friend . . . It was fairly transparent, he says, and because they lived in a tiny town, everyone knew everyone and the jig was up pretty quickly. Needless to say, circumstances like this can make it even more difficult to deal with your own mental illness.

A lot of it comes down to our old friend rumination. You identify yourself as a 'mentally ill' person, you obsess over the provenance of your illness, you find the finger pointing firmly at your own family. It's not necessarily even the case – although mental illness can be genetic, experts say that there's no real way of knowing where it comes from. Some conditions are more likely to be passed on than others – for example, the risk for bipolar in the general population is around 1 per cent, which is fairly small, but for those who have a first-degree relative with it, this can shoot up to 10 per cent. My grandmother was never formally diagnosed, but I've spoken at length to my dad about it, and there are a few pretty striking similarities between our behaviours. Likewise, my mum has never sought extended help for her anxiety or OCD, but there are certain behaviours and compulsions that mirror each other fairly closely.

It can lead to a level of resentment, if I'm honest. I've had moments where I blame my parents for my mental illness and wondered why they had me – not in an 'UGH, I WISH I'D NEVER BEEN BORN, slamming-my-bedroom-door' way, but in a genuine 'You-probably-could-have-saved-yourselves-a-lot-of-hassle-if-you'd-thought-about-it' way. I'm not judging them, obviously, and I'm certainly glad I'm here, but I have felt irritated by my own birth on more than one occasion. I've felt angry that my family have seemingly passed on this horrible burden to me, as if mental illness isn't an accident of birth but some kind of evil-stepmother curse they purposefully decided to bestow upon me.

It's not like it doesn't go the other way too, though; my mum has expressed feelings of guilt about my childhood – worries that either she didn't do enough or somehow 'caused' my mental health problems. I worry too that it could happen when I have kids, and other than the fact I'm supremely selfish it's the one thing that really puts me off becoming a mother. It doesn't help that most of the people I've been with for significant periods have also been mentally ill to varying degrees; together we could create some kind of horrible amalgam of mental illnesses.

The sense that something so horrible might be biological destiny was something I struggled with for several years. I felt trapped, tethered to my family in a way that didn't feel altogether voluntary. I felt that they represented my inability to escape my mental illness; no matter what I tried, I would always have bipolar, and I would always be tied to my family because of it. My genetics had betrayed me; so, subsequently, had my family.

At the end of the day this kind of thinking is fruitless, on both a parent's part and a child's. Did I inherit my grandmother's bipolar, or my mother's anxiety? Maybe. But maybe not. It could have been an accident of birth; I could have been pushed to the edge of sanity by a particular event; it could have just been bad luck. And even if it was my genetic destiny to be mentally ill, there's no point blaming my family; it's hardly something they deliberately foisted upon me. And, at the end of the day, no matter where my mental illness came from, only one person is responsible for managing it: me.

How to live with your family without killing yourself – or them

Beyond selfhood and rumination and all of the more concep-tual, identity-bound stuff, there's something perhaps more pressing to deal with: the practicality of living with someone when you're mentally ill. Being in a family home is often different to more casual living arrangements like a student house or sharing with friends, mainly because there's a whole different set of expectations.

I don't know about anybody else, but in my experience the level of solitude I managed to sustain in shared houses was just not possible in a family home. Things like going out when you feel like it, having people over, eating what and when you want – they all seem fairly straightforward when you're an adult, but when you live in a family home they're not always thought of in quite the same way. (If you're reading this and you've not left home yet: you have a lot to look forward to.)

It's a double-edged sword, really; having someone there to talk to during mealtimes or quietly watch TV with can be really comforting when you're feeling low or anxious. It can be nice simply to have the company, and also to have somebody who can curb your desire to hibernate.

It can also be very annoying. Sometimes, I think, being alone is kind of vital; when you're depressed you naturally withdraw, and you also need time to recharge following social situations, which are exhausting and difficult. A family home does, of course, provide some level of isolation – it's not like you're being constantly forced to be cheery and outgoing – but your ability to be so solitary is definitely limited.

It can also be hard if you're not in a place where you can talk about how you're feeling. Maybe you don't want to tell your parents because you know they'd react badly, for example; or maybe you just don't have the energy or the words to talk about how down or anxious you're feeling. Living in such close quarters with somebody can make this hard. Keeping up a front socially can be manageable; before I started writing about mental health so much, I had colleagues and acquaintances who would be genuinely surprised when I told them I had depressive periods. They never would have guessed because smiling and laughing and having a drink is manageable in periods of several hours. It's surprisingly easy to pretend you're OK in the short term.

It's not sustainable all the time, though, and it absolutely does and will sneak out at home. Home is also where you're most comfortable, hopefully, and so you're quite often the most *you* when you're there; no pretence.

As you can see, there are a fair few forces at work here – trying to stay sociable and bearable around your family, maybe trying to keep things from them a little, trying to carve out your own space for peace and quiet – and they can often make for a weird mix. For me, juggling these things has led to arguments, major fallings-out, a horribly strained living environment and increased anxiety. So here is my guide to avoiding these things, and living with your family as harmoniously as you possibly can.

- **Carve out your own little space**

    Carving out a little bit of peaceful, tranquil space can really help if you need to escape a fractious living situation. Being at home with your parents might mean that you have limited power over redecorating, but make your room as lovely as you can. Buy a nice duvet set, some rugs or some fairy lights, some cool posters, pretty photo frames or some cushions for your bed; get a bookcase and fill it with your favourite books. And none of this has to be expensive – it can all be bought fairly cheaply in high-street shops.

    Basically, do whatever you can to create a space where you feel comfortable, safe and happy. It might not seem like a big thing, but having somewhere you can escape to that automatically makes you feel calmer can really help if you're having a bad time in terms of arguments, or if you feel like you want to get away from pretending to be OK and just relax. It was hard for me to achieve this kind of space as a teenager – my mum's anxieties meant I couldn't use things like candles or incense in case I burned the house down, and the furthest I really got with making my room my own was sticking some pictures on my wall. But since leaving home I have started to appreciate the value of a nice space that makes me feel secure.

Assert this space

Asserting the right to access this space without question is the hard part. Sometimes you can't just say, 'Sorry, I need some space'; even as an adult, your motives can be questioned, your thoughts analysed, your intentions taken as an insult. It can be hard to express that it isn't a slight on the people you need space from, and that it's just for you.

If you can, then that's great. Just say: 'I need some time to chill out on my own' – and go do your thing. Obviously, it's better if you have the kind of living arrangement in which your space and autonomy are respected in this way, but it's not always that easy. So, if not, you can lie: 'I'm going to read my book'; or, 'I have something to do for school/uni/work and I need some quiet'; or, 'I have a bit of a headache so I'm going to take a paracetamol and hang out in my room'. These are all totally reasonable excuses to want to be alone, and are fairly likely to be unquestioned.

Communicate as best you can

Again, communicating with your family can be awkward and difficult or, at worst, impossible. If you can, tell them how you're feeling. If they already know your diagnosis or know that you struggle; that's great. Talk to them about it as best you can or write them an email, perhaps. Try, in whatever small way you can, to tell them how you're feeling or what help you need.

● **Establish house rules**

This is *such* boring advice. No nice 'buy yourself some fairy lights' tips here, let me tell you. It is, however, pretty useful, so listen up.

Talk to your parents and/or siblings, and try to lay down some rules on both sides. Tell them you're happy to give and take (because compromise is basically the key to successful co-living): you'll do the washing up, if they respect your need for at least an hour alone a day; you'll do some hoovering in exchange for them letting you have your own space. If you can, try to clearly assert what it is that you want to get out of living together, and let them know that you're willing to both work hard and meet them halfway in order to achieve it.

If things are clear and everybody knows where they stand, arguments over issues like whose turn it is to wash up or do the laundry can be pretty much avoided. Cleaning rotas can help here; again, boring, unglamorous advice, but the little domestic strains that family life brings really can add up when you're already feeling unstable or ill. Take steps to avoid this!

The challenges of being a carer

Being mentally ill is hard; so is being a carer. Worrying about someone constantly, closely monitoring their moods, even as you try desperately not to, picking them up when things go wrong . . . It's an underestimated vocation and it can be aggravating, irritating, frustrating and rewarding in equal measure.

Having been on both sides of the fence, in varying degrees, I feel like I have a fairly nuanced understanding of the challenges of being a carer. Caring for my anxious mum didn't require excessive amounts of effort, and it was nothing like what some children go through when looking after mentally ill parents, but it was still tough at times. And looking after various depressed partners has also proved to be difficult in ways I couldn't have anticipated beforehand, despite my own experience.

The thing that nobody wants to say about mental illness is that it can often be really annoying. I know I'm frustrating when I'm depressed: cancelling plans at the last minute, blowing hot and cold with friends – alternating between needy and distant with alarming regularity. As I've said elsewhere, I'm also very *irritable* at almost every stage of a cycle: when depressed, I find the presence of other people incredibly difficult to bear; when manic I find myself resenting people for their slowness, their perceived lack of enthusiasm, their unwillingness to just keep up with me.

It must be unbearably difficult to love me. After I dropped out of university and moved back in with my mum, I spent a solid six months lying on the sofa; I'd get up, refuse to change out of my pyjamas, lie on the sofa all day sleeping and looking at my phone and then go to bed again. I didn't help around the house, I never once cooked her a meal or made her a cup of tea, I never did my own laundry and I only did the washing up under extreme duress. When manic, I've gone weeks or months without calling her or, alternatively,

I've phoned her up when living on the other side of the country to ramble on endlessly about some harebrained plan I had to make money or to start a new course or to relocate, and then promptly stopped replying to her messages. It must have caused her unspeakable stress and worry. It must have been awful, and I can probably never apologise enough. And the worst thing, of course, is that there's always the possibility that I'll do it all again. I'll never be 'cured' because mental illness has no 'cure', and so the cycle endlessly churns on with no end in sight.

When I spoke to my mum about how it's been for her, the one thing she stressed was *patience* – having the patience and the insight to know that the person you love is simply going through a hard time and needs your help, despite their problematic behaviour or despite the fact that they might be pushing you away. While they might seem like a totally different person – maybe more snappy or meaner or just flatter, less outgoing – they're not. They're the same person you always loved, who you laughed and had in-jokes and fun with. To nurse someone through an episode of poor mental health is to have the faith – and yes, again, the patience – to know that those things will happen again.

It's important to note that patience doesn't mean giving someone a free pass, though; if someone puts you down or argues with you over nothing or just straight up insults you, you are under no obligation to just let it go. Illness can make someone difficult, but it doesn't excuse any and all behaviour. So sternness can come in too; or at the very least assertiveness.

There's an interesting debate here around autonomy and mental illness. At what point can you feasibly force somebody to do something they may not want to do, but that's best for them? At what point, for example, do you absolutely insist that they go to a doctor about medication or therapy? When can you sit someone down and sternly tell them that yes, they are going to therapy this week and no, you don't care if they don't want to go? When do you force someone to take a walk, or start eating better or to get out of bed?

My mum has taken two routes: respecting my desires, even if they are counterintuitive and self-destructive, and forcing me to do things for what she saw as the greater good. Both approaches have had mixed results. Respecting what I wanted meant allowing me to lie in bed all day and eat four packets of cream buns, which was not particularly helpful. From my point of view, I had no reason to change my behaviour – I'd dropped out, and so I had no responsibilities and, in my mind, no future. My mother didn't put her foot down, and I certainly didn't *want* to change, so why would I bother? The nebulous, superficial concept of 'happiness' just wasn't a strong enough motivator to get me out of my pyjamas.

Then again, the 'I'm-going-to-march-you-down-to-the-doctor's-office-*right-now*' strategy wasn't a particularly effective one either. As I've said, I've found my mum's pushiness with matters of mental health rather overbearing at times. So, while being forced to go to therapy was probably good for me in the long run, it drove a wedge between us for a time. I felt she was interfering with my life far more than she had any right to; she felt I was irresponsible with my mental health, seeing my refusal of help as immaturity rather than the pure terror it was actually borne of.

Of course, she was right to encourage me to go to therapy; I needed it. She was also right to tell me to get dressed, to drink more water and to leave the house every once in a while. She's probably right about a lot of the decisions I've made as a stable adult, things I've done when I've been medicated and therapised and happy. Unfortunately, though, forcing me to do those things isn't within her remit. It's not that she'd *want* to dictate what I'd do most of the time – in fact, she's always been very supportive of my often very weird life choices – but that line becomes impossibly blurred when it comes to illness.

So, how, as a carer, do you know where to draw the line between letting someone get on with their – perhaps, very poor – decisions and stopping them from acting on what you think might be some incredibly dangerous ones? The standard answer – *when they could cause serious harm to themselves or to others* – is impossibly reductive. As we know, there are plenty of ways you can cause 'serious harm' to yourself that fall under the broad umbrella of 'socially acceptable', and the likelihood that you are going to harm another person – which, of course, *would* warrant intervention – is actually very small.

Navigating the situation takes time, and is often a case of one step forward and two back. If you interfere too much, try to step back. If you feel like you're being too passive, try to involve yourself – carefully! – with treatment plans or support structures. Will you fuck up? Probably. Will it be OK, though? Almost certainly.

Friends

In my experience, friendships are less complicated than family relationships. Or, at least, they're complicated in a different way. A relationship of some kind with your family is more or less inevitable; a relationship with a friend is opt-in. This means a different kind of closeness; you've chosen to be friends, after all, and so you have to be more gentle with the relationship, more tentative. Friends have no reason to stand by you other than loyalty or love. As such, they can cut you off in a way your family never would, even if they sometimes should.

It's hard to tell where my difficult personality ends and my mental illness starts, but, either way, it's no surprise that I have lost a lot of friends. Being weird is not easy. It's not easy for anyone, even the mentally healthy. Liking different things to everybody else – or being a different *kind* of person to everybody around you – is unspeakably lonely. You feel as if nobody could ever understand you, and in most cases you're right. You like the wrong things the wrong amount. You manage to say the worst possible thing at any given moment, so that you spend most of your time thinking, Why the fuck did I just say that? The friendships you do forge tend to be very intense by necessity, and that brings a whole new raft of issues onto the table.

So, as both a weird person and a person whose mental health problems make them even weirder, my friendships have been a rather slapdash affair. I've got better at making friends as I've got older, only marginally better at keeping them. And, predictably, most of the major fallings-out I *have* had as an adult have been down to my mental health problems.

The intense friendships I form when I'm manic, and the level of sociability I'm able to maintain at that point, often fall by the wayside when I come back down to earth. If I'm depressed, I won't go out, I won't see anybody; I'll do nothing but the bare minimum. The last time I was so depressed I couldn't do anything I was lucky enough to have two friends who nursed me through it. I was pretty shitty to them, if I'm honest – at one point I deleted my Facebook account, stopped returning their texts and ignored all calls – and they still persevered. Many others, perhaps rightly, have not.

Then there were my uni friends, who I've already mentioned, who literally stepped over me as if our relationships were just a heavy-handed metaphor, and my school friends, of whom there were very few. But what about friends from my second time at uni, I hear you ask? I can't say there were any bad experiences or problematic friendships there, but that's only because I kept to myself mostly, closeting myself away in a house I shared with an unsuitable boyfriend. So, until I was about twenty-three, I had very few real friends. There were a couple here and there, of course, some incredibly close ones, but I never had a 'group'. Like many things, a big social circle seemed out of reach to me; I was too weird to fit in anywhere, slightly too insane to ever be part of the *Friends*-esque capers of my dreams.

For once, though, there's a happy end to this story. Unlike many areas of my life, which still require daily hard work, my social life has finally slotted into place. I put it down to two things: my best friend and the friends I met when I moved to London. The latter are a group of intelligent, interesting and creative people who are all either deeply empathetic or have experience of their own mental health struggles. I'm able to say, 'Sorry, I can't come to the party because I've had a really bad panic attack' in the knowledge that they're not rolling their eyes behind my back. I can tell them about my moods, and my past, and they're fine with it. They don't, as many people do, fetishise my mental illness; things I've done when manic, though often acknowledged as the great anecdotes they are, aren't treated like curios. To them, it's not a salacious insight into the weird world of a bipolar person. It's just me. It may not be much to ask someone not to ostracise you or act as if you're a freak, but it's rare for this to be honoured. Other people have had better experiences with groups of friends, I'm sure, but for me, just having people around is still kind of special.

As for my best friend – she, in very mawkish terms, is my soulmate. We have some of the same neuroses, she's funny, weird, dry, dark and smart in equal measure, she's as much of an attention seeker as me. She understands everything I express about my mental health problems immediately, even if it's bizarre or fucked up, and even though she herself suffers from an entirely different set of problems. She's willing to comfort me, but only up to a point, and is such a proponent of tough love that she's been responsible for innumerable successful interventions.

For people who are able to make friends normally, who aren't constantly worried about scaring people off with their mental health, having a best friend may not feel like such a big deal. Numerous partners have been baffled at the obsessive closeness of our relationship, of how intimate and romantic we are when our friendship has always been entirely platonic. I think it's because mental illness can wear you down to a point where you absolutely wholeheartedly believe that something inherent within you is broken or wrong. Everything seems to confirm it; lack of friends, maybe, or social anxiety or relationships breaking down or failing to launch to begin with. You become stoic about it; that's just the way it is, I guess. I'm just not like other people.

So when you find someone who somehow *just fucking gets it,* who understands and empathises and actually genuinely cares, it can make your friendship deeper and more intimate and more fulfilling than anything else in life. I'm certainly not one for sentimental stories of personal transformation, where someone goes from deep depression to inspiring OK-ness because they met someone on the bus or they fell in love or whatever; I find them mawkish, and I don't think they address or understand on any kind of meaningful level what it means to be mentally ill. But for me, it's not hyperbole to say that a friendship like this can save your life. It absolutely can.

Building a support network

So yes, finding friendship like this is hard. It took me 23 years before I had a 'group of friends' in any real way because it was so hard to find and retain friends who are willing to stick around while you deal with your problems. There are, however, a few things you can do to build a network and keep it alive.

- **Be honest**

  There is absolutely no way you are going to maintain a successful friendship if you're not honest. I'm not saying you have to share your mental health status with acquaintances or gig buddies or people you sometimes talk to in the kitchen at work. But in terms of close friendships, my policy is always that honesty is best. There's no separation between my mental illness and me – we come as a package.

The best kind of friendships tell you something essential about yourself that you couldn't explore or discover on your own. In order to achieve that level of rewarding friendship, though, you need to give yourself up a bit – and that involves being wholeheartedly you, brain zaps, panic attacks and all.

Likewise, being honest is also necessary once you have this type of communication and understanding. I've gone for long periods without telling my best friend that I'm deeply depressed, and there was absolutely no benefit. Maybe I didn't want to worry her; maybe I hoped that if I didn't mention it then it would go away. Spoiler alert: it does not just go away. Telling your friends where you're at, even if it's hard to talk about it, will likely help. At the very least, they can distract you with cat gifs and links to articles and cups of coffee and maybe make you forget, for an hour at a time, that you're sad.

Get online

There's more on this later in the book (see pp. 176–90), but there are lots of communities online that can help with your mental health – forums, specialist websites, Twitter . . . There are tonnes of people out there with similar conditions to yours – people who just understand, people who will listen to you talk about how you feel and offer you genuine advice and help. The dynamic is different to a 'real-life' friend in lots of ways – chatting to someone over email isn't the same as having a cup of tea with someone, for example – but it's no less valid, especially if it helps you cope.

For me, a big community on Twitter has been a saving grace on more than one occasion. Even when I'm not actually talking about mental health, there's a constant stream of pleasant conversation, shared articles and the minutiae of other people's lives, not to mention the active support and advice I've had regarding mental health. And this has been a real comfort to me. It may not be for you – you may not feel comfortable sharing your thoughts online – but it's worth trying.

• Get out and *do stuff*

There are two benefits to leaving the house and doing things. One: you will get closer to your friends, or maybe make new ones. Two: doing things is good for your mental health.

Not leaving the house is not healthy. It's understandable, sometimes unavoidable, but it's certainly not healthy. It exacerbates existing problems by failing to acknowledge them; it's stubbornly refusing to admit that the real world is anything other than an irritating subplot in the story that is your inner life. And the more you stay inside, the harder it is to get back out there. I've gone to parties or the pub after a few solid weeks of staying in alone and found my voice weak and small, my throat constricted and clogged with terror and indecision, absolutely empty of things for me to say. My interactions on those occasions, it's safe to say, were not particularly successful. Instead of being fulfilling and fun, they actually strengthened my desire to stay in and see nobody, thus starting the cycle again.

If you join a club or go to the pub with some colleagues or meet up with your mate for a coffee, you will be opening yourself up to new experiences, for a start, which is always good. You'll get a bit of low-pressure social interaction, which is obviously great, and you'll be stimulated, physically and intellectually. You'll also get some fresh air, you'll be moving around and you won't be in bed, which is the most important thing. Plus, getting *back* into bed after a few hours out of the house is probably the single greatest thing a human can experience.

Practical ways to help someone with a mental illness

Lots of books about mental health will tell you to *love* and *care* for your friends in the vaguest possible way. But when I need to help someone out I'm not really interested in juggling *ideas* and *concepts*; I want cold, hard facts. I want lists of things I can *do*. I want to be useful. I actually want to support them. Do I want to instil a boyfriend with an ephemeral sense of joy via inspirational macro? No. I want to help him get out of bed.

So, rather than give you the kind of airy fairy advice you might have received before, here is a (definitely not definitive) list of things you can do to practically help a friend who's feeling depressed.

● **Take them outside**

As we've already seen, going out is good. Leaving the house

is good. Fresh air is really good. It isn't going to cure someone of depression, obviously, but it can help temporarily lift their mood – make them feel more alert and awake and fresh.

They will probably not want to go. They will most likely object to your suggestion that they leave the house. This is a time where being insistent can actually help, though, because you're encouraging someone to do a low-effort thing that has moderately high returns. Every time someone suggests it to me I initially refuse, but when I'm eventually forced into going, it really helps. I might be a whiny little baby about it while it's happening, of course, but I still do it – and once it's done I appreciate it.

In practice:
- Find somewhere peaceful, nice or scenic to walk; a place that's quiet and fresh and undemanding like the beach, a river or a park where you can have a wander.
- Make them a picnic and eat it outside (this may only work in the summer, or if you live somewhere where it isn't constantly raining).
- Go out for a cup of coffee or a drink. Walk there and back.

● **Do some chores**

A really sucky thing about depression, amongst many other things, is its ability to render you completely incapable of completing normal tasks. When it's really bad, even showering seems like an impossible mission, as I've said, let alone doing laundry or opening mail or cleaning your house. Helping someone to do one, or several, of these things is probably the most practical thing you can do. It's also one of the easiest because housework can be broken down into loads of much smaller tasks that can be done as and when. Having a tidy and clean house can really help to improve someone's mood too.

I recently went across London to pick up a prescription for a friend who couldn't manage it himself. It took maybe an hour and a half out of my day and a minimal amount of energy; I sat on the Tube for an hour, I walked to the pharmacy, I talked to the pharmacist and I left. No big deal for me. But for my friend, it was. Not only had I managed to do something practical for him, something that had desperately needed to be done, but I'd also shown that I cared enough to make that effort – which, however briefly, made him feel a little less miserable.

In practice:
► Make an avoided phone call on their behalf. This could be to make a doctor's appointment or to call a plumber, for example; something small that they've been putting off.
► Go through their unopened mail with them and sort it into piles: things to action, things to file, things to throw away. Help them shred unwanted letters.
► Do some laundry for them – you could combine this with the walking idea and wander down to a laundrette with them or you could simply go round to their home and shove a load in the washing machine.
► Do some washing up. Keeping up with this is something

I struggle with even when I'm not depressed. Having someone come in and help me with it or with other cleaning can make a big difference.

▸ Take out their trash.
▸ Help them with admin stuff: taxes, bills, organising appointments. Even if you just sit with them while they do things themselves, rather than actually taking over, you can provide some vital support.

Food, food, food

A healthy relationship with food can be one of the first things to go when you're having a crisis. You either eat nothing out of lethargy or you binge on crisps at 2am. Hot meals? What the hell is a hot meal? Five a day? Lol nope.

In practice:

▸ Take them out for dinner. It doesn't have to be super expensive, but dragging them out of the house and making them eat some delicious and healthy food can make a big impact on mood.
▸ Invite them round for a meal. Make everything cosy and warm and nice – make them feel at home.
▸ Order a takeaway, either remotely or to share with them.
▸ Do some grocery shopping for them and cook with them.
▸ Bake them some healthy treats.
▸ Try one of the new food-delivery services, which select healthy meals and send you a weekly box with ingredients and recipes in them. Your friend might not be up for cooking every day, but if they are, then this can be

a way to show you care *and* make sure they're eating enough vegetables.

- **Make them a care package**

A friend of mine, who is severely depressed, receives a care package from someone every month. He packs it full of books and sweets and little Post-it notes with in-jokes and cute messages written on them. She's always so pleased and proud and comforted by the fact that someone repeatedly takes the time and effort to send her things to make her feel good.

The care package is super personalised, so the list below is just an example, but it can be a helpful and thoughtful way of showing that you know them, that you care and that you're just *there*, especially if the person in question is in hibernation mode and doesn't want to go out. It doesn't have to be a monthly thing, of course, but the fact that it lifts my friend's mood so obviously and dramatically, even for a little while, makes me a firm advocate. And if you can't afford, or haven't got the time or resources, to put a whole box together, you can always order them something online too.

In practice:
- Something that tastes good – nice teabags, something you've baked.
- Something that smells good – candles, incense, perfume, bath salts, body lotion.
- Something that feels good – a blanket, some fluffy socks, new PJs
- Something to occupy their mind – a book of crosswords,

word searches or Sudokus (these are my nerdiest and best coping strategies), a magazine or comic (basically something untaxing and simple).

- **Listen**

This is super easy. So easy, in fact, there are only four steps.

In practice:
- ► Shut up.
- ► Listen.
- ► Ask them what they want or need from you.
- ► Do that thing.

This isn't an exhaustive list, of course, and it's important to remember that no matter what you do, you're not going to make your friends not-depressed. These are just a few practical ways in which you can make your friends feel loved, attended to, maybe temporarily relieved of stress and depression.

CHAPTER 7

THE INTERNET

I t's hard to think of one aspect of my life that isn't inextricably linked to the Internet. I've met several serious partners on the Internet and all of my friends. I got a career in writing from the Internet, a job, this book. I learned how to be myself online; I became a feminist because of online discourse, reading reams of badly scanned PDFs of essays and books and papers that have shaped the way I think about myself and the world. My self-image, the conception I have of my own body, the way I inhabit myself, are all connected to my online presence.

It is no surprise, then, that there is a complex relationship between my mental health and the Internet. It's acted variously as a trigger, an emotional crutch, a lifeline, an addiction and a distraction. It's exacerbated problems that already exist and probably created new ones, but it's also been a vital source of comfort, knowledge, insight and understanding. I just can't overstate the impact it's had on my life.

Like most people my age, I first started using the Internet when I was about twelve. I would go on a few AOL chatrooms, play Neopets, all the standard early 2000s stuff that anyone younger than me probably views as a terrifyingly ancient relic.

And they'd be right to – the Internet speeds then truly were horrifying.

Then, one summer when I was about fourteen, my mum started working long hours and I was forced to spend long days alone during the holidays. Most of my school friends lived nowhere near me; and those who did, I was more interested in avoiding than seeing. So instead of reading or writing or doing something productive, like leaving the house or seeing friends, I did what any self-respecting introvert would do: I went online.

It started in small spurts. I'd go online for a few hours before wandering back to the living room to flick through books or watch TV. This was before the days of laptops, of course, so I was confined to one tiny room, using an unwieldy desktop device; I couldn't multitask. At first, I found the room claustrophobic; my family referred to the room as 'the study', which, to me, conjures images of a big desk and a well-organised pen holder and some nice paintings on the walls. In reality, it was little more than a cupboard, with bookshelves lining the walls, making the room even smaller and more oppressive, and piles of books that had to be ritualistically navigated before you could reach the computer and log on.

Then I started going on for longer bursts – five or six hours at a time. By the end of the holidays, I was getting up at 8am to log on to my slow-running desktop, only logging off to go to bed at 10pm. I started getting up in the night to go online too, sneaking past my mum's bedroom careful not to wake her, to sit in the blue glow of a screen. When she got suspicious about my nocturnal activity, she'd check to see how hot the top of the computer tower was, so I would wrap ice in a towel and place it carefully atop the tower to keep it cool.

Once, she took the keyboard to work with her so I couldn't go online, but so dedicated to MSN Messenger and Myspace was I that I painstakingly used the mouse and a character map of the alphabet to type my messages. It took forever, obviously, but it was worth it – because I was *connected*, somehow, to other people.

Perhaps the most obvious reason I found so much solace online comes down, yet again, to my innate weirdness. Though my tastes erred towards the esoteric compared to what went on in my tiny suburban village, they're certainly on the tame end of the scale when it comes to the Internet, so it was easy to find people who shared my interests and philosophies. Feminism and left-wing politics were frowned upon by my peers, most of whom were capital and lower-case Conservatives, but on forums and chatrooms I found people who shared my points of view. My obsessive enthusiasm about the things that I loved was normally mocked, but online it was encouraged. There were thousands of tiny silos of people, all of whom loved the same things as me to the same degree and who understood what it was like to be strange and alienated and lost in the world. It still amazes me now, scrolling through my Twitter feed and hanging out with my Internet-sourced friends, that there are so many people who get me and share the nichest of niche interests with me. When I first gained access to this world, it was genuinely mind-blowing. It felt radical and exciting and important – because it was.

Because I had this space, which felt so uniquely my own, I tentatively started thinking and talking and writing about how I was feeling. The way I expressed myself wasn't great, I have to admit; as I've already said, I was into Morrissey and Sylvia Plath, and I romanticised my misery because I had no other way of conceptualising it. I mainly wrote bad poetry which I posted on Myspace and which received lots of compliments – though, weirdly and completely inexplicably, all from the many older men who were attempting to populate my Top 8.

To have people tell me – and, perhaps more spuriously, to have numerous Internet quizzes tell me – that I might be mentally ill, rather than just sad or bored or a teenager, meant that for the first time I felt as if my experiences were valid and worthwhile. Hearing others say, 'Oh yeah, I have that too. I feel those things too,' gave me the confidence and strength to push forward in seeking help, and to understand that I wasn't just some awful attention-seeking brat.

As I've got older and more self-aware, the Internet has played less of a role in my self-discovery and more of a role in self-care. I use my main Twitter account for promoting my writing, mainly, and telling dumb jokes about my cat. But I have a second, locked account where I tell a select group of people about my problems, I discuss my day, look into their worlds and feel a sense of deep comfort. It's a tiny community that harks back to the early days of the Internet – oversharing, tweets about the minutiae of someone's day, their dinner, their boyfriends or their jobs. This constant stream of banality has got me through so many bad days. Most of the people I talk to online in this context have experience of mental illness too, so a few rapid-fire tweets about a panic attack or an urge to self-harm are quickly met with genuine understanding, reassurance and practical advice. During a particularly bad panic attack, several people distracted me by talking to me about their days and one sent me a breathing exercise via a gif. It helped a lot.

Knowing that there are people a few clicks away who really understand mental illness and are willing, at any time of day, to talk to me about it, is incredibly reassuring. Mostly, I use my private Twitter account to talk about how I just had a totally delicious orange juice or I've had a wank or my bank account is overdrawn but I'm feeling kind of ¯_(ツ)_/¯ about it, but it's a tiny oasis of calm and support in an otherwise chaotic life.

How the Internet Can Hinder

All this is not to say that the Internet is wholly a force for good. My obsessive checking of Myspace as a teenager, or twelve-hour stints online, were not – and are still not – healthy. Shutting myself indoors, doing nothing but watching Netflix and sending tweets is not healthy. It's very easy to become obsessed with the Internet when you're depressed in particular because it's so accessible, so perfectly designed for introversion and escapism. I don't have to speak to a real-life person for days if I don't want to. When I first started working as a freelance writer I worked from home, and I would go days and days without seeing another human being. The most face-to-face contact or conversation I had was saying 'Thanks' to the guy who brought my online shopping to my door; occasionally, I would venture to the corner shop to buy some cigarettes and talk to the guy who runs the shop. It wasn't healthy behaviour. I was steadfastly attempting to avoid reality – and having contact with both real-life and online-only friends, pretty much twenty-four hours a day, facilitated that.

This, as my ice-packed desktop tower could tell you, can be a problem. A paper released by NHS England in 2014 suggested that young people and teenagers who spend too much time online are 'at risk of developing anxiety and depression' and while, with my lack of medical expertise, I'd be loath to ascribe any particular factor to the development of a mental illness, I can say that in my own experience, it has definitely served to exacerbate my problems.

How to Stay Safe Online

Browse Tumblr, Twitter or just Google a few vague phrases and you'll come across blogs and forums dedicated to self-harm, as well as thousands more to eating disorders. They are support communities designed to help people, and are more often than not harmless.

However, one of the major problems for me online is the huge abundance of pro-self-harm and pro-suicide communities. These have come under far more scrutiny in recent years, with several cases being reported of people being encouraged to kill themselves by faceless Internet strangers. This is unlikely to happen to you; the number of people who want to help, or at least to listen, far outweighs those who want to push you towards suicide. So, worrying as these cases are, they're an anomaly. The real problem is that the sites exist at all – sites that tell you how to cut and where, which foods to avoid and how to hide uneaten meals, even which combination of pills will most effectively and least painlessly kill you. And it was sites such as these that pushed me closer and closer towards suicide; they helped me formulate plans, made me feel as if my deep, despairing depression was a reasonable lifestyle choice. It seems hypocritical for me to tell you not to visit these sites, but seriously: *do not visit them*.

• Install a website blocker

In an ideal world, it would be great to tell you to just turn your computer off when you're feeling tempted to visit pro-self-harm or pro-suicide websites. Unfortunately, we do not live in an ideal world, and to give you that advice would be incredibly impractical of me. So, instead, I'd recommend that you install a website blocker. There are about a million different options – browser plugins or programs you down-load to your computer – some stricter than others. Some will block certain websites for a small period of time – say, twenty minutes or half an hour – but some are really strict, and even if you turn your computer off and on again, you can't access the sites until the time is up. Lots of these apps also make it impossible for you to uninstall them while a block is on, which means you pretty much have no way around it.

It's not a perfect solution, of course, and you may not have the willpower to always click the button to block the sites, but if you can feel yourself nearing the terrible tunnel-vision phase of an episode, they can really help. They're also a great tool for improving productivity when you're feeling down, distracted and unable to concentrate, so are worth looking into for more than one reason.

• Change your privacy settings

Sometimes, posting about how bad you're feeling seems like the only thing you can possibly do. You want to express yourself; you want to share your pain. I often find myself typing and deleting cry-for-help tweets over and over again, or feeling this odd and implacable urge to just *say something* to articulate how I feel. But in a public setting, like a public Twitter account or Facebook page, it is rarely a good idea.

This is not advice I give without vast prior experience. I'm better at it now, but for the past ten years I have been absolutely terrible when it comes to posting miserable things – mostly vague, mostly useless – when depressed. I've also been guilty of posting frequently, and embarrassingly, when I've been manic. It's worst when I'm psychotic, but just being slightly high is bad enough because then I'm prone to posting maybe 100 tweets a day. Afterwards, I generally feel embarrassed, and I mostly delete them.

When I look back at most of these posts, especially on Facebook, the comments are mainly from people who, in hindsight, I know didn't really care about how I was. They were interested because I was being vague and odd, because they were nosy and they wanted gossip, because they wanted to barge in and feel important. If any of these people had cared, they would have contacted me privately, which they rarely did, or would have done something more practical. They would have asked me if I needed help, or they would have contacted a member of my family or a close friend to check up on me. They never did.

Privacy settings are another – albeit imperfect – solution. Facebook has settings that allow you to tailor an audience for each of your posts; you can share something publicly or with your friends, or choose specific people to hide your posts from. When I feel as if I'm getting depressed or manic, or am aware that I'm having a particularly bad episode, I change the default audience setting to 'Only Me'. If I want people to see the post, I have to manually change it, giving me a small pause to think about what I'm saying, who I'm choosing to share it with and whether or not it needs to go out to 600+ people, many of whom I don't even really know. They very rarely do.

This is a lot harder if you use Twitter, because there are pretty much only two options, locked or public, and locking your account doesn't prevent people who already follow you from seeing your posts. At times when I feel really awful, I deactivate my Twitter account to stop myself from compulsively tweeting. You can deactivate for thirty days before your account, followers and tweets are deleted permanently, which is plenty of time to consider how you feel and hopefully move away from a desire to compulsively post.

• Keep an eye on how you're using the Internet

Try to be aware of how much you're using the Internet and what you're doing once you're online. Are you using it in moderation or are you sitting up until 4am and going to work or school bleary-eyed and exhausted? Are you chatting with friends, blogging or reading interesting things or are you visiting websites about self-harm and suicide? Are your posts generally positive or neutral in tone or are you finding yourself increasingly posting negative, pessimistic things?

If you keep an eye on the way you're using the Internet, it can really help you monitor both your moods and any problematic behaviour that may be associated with your Internet use. This is where a mood diary can come in handy again (see p. 51). Adapt it to log your Internet use: what time are you using it? Do you log on or post when you're feeling a particular way? What are your thoughts when you're using the Internet? Writing these things down, or at least asking yourself the questions, can be a good way of discerning which behaviours are problematic and which are not.

• Don't use the Internet as a replacement for a therapist or doctor

Finding out information about your diagnosis online is good. Researching conditions before you get a diagnosis can be good too. But it's important to remember that the Internet is absolutely not a replacement for a doctor.

It's easy to find online tests that tell you whether or not you have a particular disorder; in one afternoon you can diagnose yourself with every personality disorder under the sun (and trust me, I have done this). But these tests, even if they are the same as those administered by a doctor, are not a replacement for actually seeing a professional. And some of them are not even medically sound and have absolutely no clinical basis; there is no way you can accurately diagnose yourself with them, even if they do reflect what you might be going through to some extent. They may be OK as a starting point if you're at the beginning of your mental health journey and are trying to work out what it is that you're experiencing. But you really do need to take them with a pinch of salt; see them as an additional tool in an arsenal that also includes mental healthcare professionals.

• Set phone- or computer-free time aside

Being online is great. The Internet is great. But – and bear with me on this one – so is . . . not . . . being . . . online.

I know, I know, it sounds fake. But it can be genuinely helpful.

Try to keep a healthy balance between being online and offline. It's harder than ever to draw the line between the two, especially when hanging out with friends in person is often punctuated by tiny spurts of mobile Internet use too. But if you're online more than you're offline, and time spent with your friends or family is invariably accompanied by the constant presence of your phone, then it may be wise to have a break.

You don't have to quit the Internet altogether, but try dedicating some time every day to not using a phone or computer. Before bed can be a good time for this, as research has shown that looking at a screen before you go to sleep can affect sleep quality. The charity Mind also suggest starting slowly: take ten-minute breaks from the Internet at first, then gradually build up to longer periods offline.

Temporarily deleting accounts can help here, as I said above – breaks from Twitter and Facebook at the peaks of episodes have been invaluable to me, as they've given me time and space to think about myself and my feelings, and to alter my behaviour. Breaks from the Internet also force me to go and speak to people, leave the house and do the kinds of things that normal, sane people do. And while I'm never going to be one of them, it can be nice to pretend for a bit.

How to Make Sure the Information You're Getting is Correct

One of the other major benefits of the Internet is that it makes large amounts of information available to anyone, and mostly for free. Outside of the opinion-based worlds of social media and blogging, it provides endless facts too. Textbooks, novels, academic papers, encyclopaedia entries . . . there's not much you can't find online. It can be a great resource for informing your opinion and understanding of things like medication, therapy and just the basic psychological and biological details of your own illness.

The fact that anyone can post anything they want online can be a good thing – marginalised people are given a voice and a platform previously denied to them, which is revolutionary and radical and wonderful. But it also means that people who have no real idea what they're talking about with regards to particular topics are able to write whatever they damn please about those topics, and consequently the Internet also has an awful lot of crap on it. I've had lots of interesting and empowering debates online about different aspects of mental health, but I've also seen people post potentially dangerous things, misinterpret and then disseminate incorrect ideas and sometimes straight-up lie.

So, what do you do when you're looking for information online and you don't know what to believe?

- **Visit websites you trust**

  When I'm looking for information on mental health, I have a few failsafe go-to websites. Mental health charities like

Mind, SANE, Rethink and Time to Change all provide detailed background info and tonnes of practical advice. The Mix, a website run by YouthNet, also has articles, lists and explainers aimed at young people that break down topics into basic, simple and easy-to-understand detail.

All of these sites give you verified facts about mental health in a clear, concise and, most importantly, *trustworthy* way. They are also staffed by knowledgeable, approachable teams who, should you need to get in touch, are happy to provide you with more information or clarification on particular topics. They all have a social-media presence too, so you can get in touch with them that way if you're not up for using the phone.

Double, triple, quadruple check

The information you're reading might seem correct, but before actually acting on any advice it's best to double-check that it's based on fact. First: Google it. Has anyone else on the whole Internet said it? If so, who? Was it someone reputable and trustworthy or are there just a few badly written blogs?

If you're still not sure, contact a charity or mental health professional, especially if the advice is something you're likely to put into practice and has the potential to cause more harm than good.

Don't be afraid to take it offline

It's nice to have the Internet to help you with even the smallest of queries, and it can be especially empowering if you're nervous about talking about your mental health problems out loud or in real life. But don't be scared to take your worries offline.

A GP, counsellor, psychiatrist or psychologist is, on balance, actually better equipped to deal with your questions than a stranger on the Internet. Their treatment or approach may not always be perfect; nobody's denying that. But they are trained and experienced and have qualifications that allow them to give you the advice and help that you need.

* * *

I've still not really shaken off my obsession with the Internet. When I'm depressed or manic, my online life is one of the first things to be affected. I post too much or go off the grid for too long; I ramble and obsess and stay up until 6am, looking at stupid memes or totally exhausting Netflix's supply of serial-killer documentaries. Fairly normal online behaviours become pathological, in other words.

But what I have done in more recent years is to take a more mindful approach to how I use the Internet. This has certainly been challenging, not least because I'm an online journalist: I research articles online and I am an embarrassingly prolific Twitter user. My friends use the Internet in the same way as me, so we organise events and nights out and trips to the pub online. It is part of my life in such a way that I barely think about it any more. The Internet is no longer the separate 'space' it was ten or fifteen years ago; rather, it is an extension of the tangible physical reality that I exist in every day.

But as with anything else, moderation is key. Drinking is also a huge part of most people's lives; they'll have a glass of wine with dinner, or a beer after a shitty day, or they'll meet their mates in the pub. That doesn't mean that their behaviours around drinking aren't moderated, though – they certainly are. Most of us know when we're drinking too much, or if we've binged when we shouldn't have, or if we're spending more hours of the day drinking or thinking about drinking than not. Internet use should be no different. Careful, mindful behaviour that takes into consideration usage and mood may seem unusual, but in an age where the line between 'real life' and the Internet is increasingly blurred and often arbitrary, it's a vital tool for good mental health.

CHAPTER 8

RECOVERY AND RELAPSE

When I'd finally recovered from my first proper breakdown, I thought I had it made. I had been psychotic, yes, but that, I believed, was a matter of circumstance; I had a little depression, sure, but I wasn't *mentally ill*. I'd recover from it fully, get back into the swing of things, return to uni and live a normal life again. I'd avoid the triggers that caused me to break down to begin with. I'd get some sleep. I wouldn't drink too much. I'd dutifully take my medication every day until I no longer needed to – or maybe even for ever. I just didn't think of mental illness as a chronic condition. I was positive, essentially.

This attitude was strengthened when I got into a 'normal' relationship with a 'normal' person. The fact that our relationship turned out to be doomed was beside the point; we did normal-people things, like going for overpriced breakfasts in cafés with exposed brick walls and saving up for a mortgage on a house. We looked at engagement rings and discussed baby names. We did things, in short, that I had no particular interest in, but that I felt were necessary parts of leading a 'normal' life. I thought these things would protect me – that a cheap vintage engagement ring was a talisman that would ward off breakdown for ever.

I was wrong, of course. And the fact that I bought so heavily into the lie made it harder to deal with when it eventually and inevitably went wrong. Recovery was supposed to be a straight line, I thought. I was supposed to start at the very bottom, nestled pathetically between the x and y axes, and slowly move up and away from it. I was supposed to keep rising – no sudden dips back down towards zero. So when that happened, it was crushing.

Studies show that diagnoses for mental illness are more complicated than we thought. There's no clearly defined 'ill' and 'not ill', 'well' or 'recovered'. It's a sliding scale, a spectrum that we all move up and down, no matter how sane we might be. So, I'm always somewhere on a scale of one to ten. It's not like I'm '6 mad' one day and '8 mad' the next – but it's a nuanced and complex and nebulous thing that just does not fit into a cut-and-dried, dichotomous binary.

And the same goes for recovery.

At first, I didn't know this. I thought 'recovery' was easy. But when is a person 'well'? What does 'well' even mean? Lots of government-endorsed studies say 'well' is when you can function at work, which seems an unsatisfactory marker to me. Not only is that bound up in all sorts of cultural expectations about what makes a person 'productive' and 'useful', but it also rings untrue for me. I've diligently shown up to work every day during the very worst episodes of mental illness I've ever had. By those standards, I was well; I was able to hold down a job – just. But I was emphatically *not* well: six of every eight hours I spent at work during that time were spent pondering suicide, I was drinking until I was sick every night and I was self-harming badly too. I wasn't well at all.

What about when I'm not suicidal, though? Day to day, I'm still affected by mental illness. As I write, I've been medication-free for a year and, aside from a few admittedly major blips, have been fairly stable and steady. I self-harm rarely. I drink far less now, especially when I'm alone. I have a job that I'm not only good at and thrive in, but that I actually, actively enjoy. Yet every day is blighted in some respect by various manifestations of bipolar: anxiety, paranoia, intense and constant intrusive thoughts, mood swings . . . By some standards, I'm absolutely not well. By others, I've 'recovered'.

I think this is what makes 'recovery' such a slippery concept; there are no real parameters by which to judge it. Charities like Mind and the Mental Health Foundation acknowledge this, and refer to recovery as a 'journey' or 'process', rather than as a fixed point in time. And this is how it should be – because there's literally no way to measure 'wellness' objectively, no way to quantify levels of mental illness with data, even if you do diligently fill in your mood diary every day.

But this vagueness made me feel disheartened with my progress. I wrongly believed that one day I'd be completely better, and that my life would resemble something that, in reality, it had never looked like to begin with. I thought 'getting better' meant everything would be perfect and nothing would go wrong ever again – and so every time something *did* go wrong, no matter how small, it felt like a crushing defeat, as I've said. This response is impractical on a number of levels – not least because small things go wrong all the time over the course of a life: sometimes you'll fuck up at work and your boss will rightfully yell at you; someone will dump you;

and you will just wake up some days in a horrible mood for no reason whatsoever. But I didn't take these as markers of a life lived fully; I saw them as dramatic missteps in my epic quest to get well.

To that end, I've pursued many things in the name of wellness: namely, medication and therapy.

Medication

I have been on so many different medications that I almost no longer remember which ones I've taken and which I haven't. I was started on SSRIs (Selective Serotonin Reuptake Inhibitors) – the classic, entry-level antidepressants. Fluoxetine and citalopram, paroxetine and sertraline; all impotent agents in the battle for my health (although citalopram made me less anxious for a while). This is not because they're useless generally, of course, but because for many years nobody listened to what I was saying about my condition. I was just on the wrong medication.

Because I have bipolar, and SSRIs are largely prescribed for unipolar depression, in some cases they made things worse. Sertraline catapulted me into a mixed state. I was incredibly agitated and antsy and had the drive of mania, but I was also despairing and angry and sad. The two competed with each other, neither one quite cancelling the other out. I did a lot of the things I would do when manic: talking endlessly at people, updating my Facebook status multiple times a day and tweeting almost constantly. The only difference was that the joyful ebullience of mania was replaced with irritability and anger; I was tweeting all the time about how *angry* I was, about how *totally fucked-up* I felt. It felt like shit. It was also really, really annoying for everyone else.

After my bipolar diagnosis I was put on an antipsychotic, quetiapine. It made me so groggy I couldn't function, and it also made me balloon in weight – I went up two dress sizes in about a month, which didn't do much for my already shaky self-esteem. That was nothing compared to the other side effects, though; I was sleeping for twelve or thirteen hours a night, then struggling to stay awake in the day. I'd sit on the bus on my way to work and often fall asleep, finding myself miles away from my office in some depot in south London, a bus driver telling me I had to get off. I'd fall asleep in meetings, and my already pretty sparse social life came to a complete standstill. All I wanted to do was sleep. And sleep I did. I'd get in from work at six-thirty or seven in the evening and immediately get into bed, not waking up until the morning, when the whole horrible cycle would start again. Had I not been employed, I have no doubt that I'd have spent twenty hours a day sleeping, and the other four in a horrible fugue state, stumbling around like a zombie.

I also discovered, at my peril, that taking my medication at the right time of day was actually imperative. I was used to winging it; it didn't really matter to me whether I took my contraception at 9am or 9pm, nor my antidepressants (though it's important to note that it's strongly encouraged that both of these are taken at a regular time). With quetiapine, however, I could not be so blasé. I forgot to take it one night when I came in from work, so having woken at 4am, I decided to take it then instead. It was a mistake. I woke up when my alarm went off completely unable to move. My legs literally didn't work, crumpling underneath me as soon as I tried to stand up. And I couldn't speak either; I tried to say something aloud to myself and a slurred jumble came out. I made my way to the toilet, which I could barely sit on, and went straight back to bed. There was no way I was getting to work.

I decided to email my boss to tell him I had flu, as there was no way I could actually explain what had happened. I typed the email very slowly. Every letter was a tiny mountain, unconquerable by my jelly brain. Finally, happy with my hand-iwork, I sent it and collapsed into a dry-mouthed sleep. Later, I found that what I had sent was indecipherable nonsense, though at least my boss could tell I wasn't throwing a sickie for no reason (even if he did probably think I was drunk or on drugs, rather than dosed up on antipsychotics).

Quetiapine did prove useful in the short term – my suicidal depression lifted fairly quickly, and my mood improved by quite some way – but the side effects were too much. I wouldn't like to speculate about my experiences with medication in general and how normal they've been, and when I spoke to friends about theirs I found a mixed bag. Some have taken antidepressants and found that they picked them up and helped them stay stable; others feel that their medication exacerbated their problems or simply didn't help. Some consider their medication a boring but vital part of their day-to-day lives; others see it as a short-term solution to lift or change their moods during a particular episode – a tiny Band Aid to cover up wounds that can be tended to more profoundly or more effectively by therapy.

The fact of the matter is, as with so many other things, it all comes down to personal experience, and equipping your-self with knowledge about medication and all it entails can help.

• What am I going to be prescribed?

The most commonly prescribed medications are antidepressants. SSRIs, as mentioned above, are likely to be the
first port of call for most doctors, though the particular
drug that is chosen for you may vary. There are a bunch
of other antidepressants: SNRIs, tricyclics, MAOIs. For
anxiety, there are also beta blockers and tranquillisers; for
bipolar, antipsychotics and anticonvulsants and lithium. So
the answer is: it depends on your diagnosis and how your
doctor feels it can best be treated.

• How do I get medication?

There is one and only one answer to this: go to see a
medical professional. Do not borrow drugs from your
friend. Do not buy drugs on the Internet. Do not self-med-
icate in any way. You need to see a doctor.

When I was finding it hard to sleep I started taking
Valium, which I'd bought off a friend who had obtained a
job lot not exactly legally. I thought it was a great idea: I
can't sleep; Valium makes me sleep. What's the problem
there? The problem was that it hadn't been prescribed for
me, and other than a brief browse of a few drug forums
and Wikipedia, I didn't know much about it. It turns out
it's extremely addictive.

When I ran out, and was unable to immediately obtain
any more, I decided to go cold turkey. I felt awful, and my
insomnia got even worse. I later went to see my psychiatrist,
who prescribed me some proper sleeping pills, which I got
via the much less risky (but marginally less thrilling) Boots
pharmacist. She knew my medical history, she had blood-

test results in front of her and she knew me and my experiences. It was much, much better than my own dodgy self-medicating, and much safer.

What will the side effects be?

The obvious answer here is that it depends what you're taking, but common side effects of antidepressants and antipsychotics can be nausea, dizziness and loss of sex drive. One particularly egregious side effect of antidepressants, which seemed to affect me more than anything else, is teeth-grinding; when I was first put on citalopram, I spent about four days grinding my teeth and clenching my jaw, resulting in a horribly sore mouth. It felt like the day after taking a bunch of ecstasy, only I had absolutely no fun throughout the entire experience.

With some meds, you may feel increased levels of depression or suicidal thoughts immediately after starting your course, which seems counterproductive, but they do – trust me – go away after a while.

The best thing to do is ask your doctor about side effects, thoroughly read and take in the literature that will come with your meds and do your research online. Do not, however, take much notice of forum posts, which are often mildly terrifying.

Lots of people have bad experiences with medication, sure, but don't let that put you off. Lots of people have good experiences too; they're just less likely to post about them online. This also goes for many of the side effects listed in the medication pamphlet: yes, sudden death syndrome might occur for some people taking the same meds as you, but it is extremely, extremely unlikely, and you are far more likely to get a boring headache for three days instead. Aripiprazole, the medication I was prescribed most recently, can apparently cause 'increased sexual interest', but also 'swelling of the mouth, face and tongue', which could have caused my love life to go in one of two very different directions. In reality, I was fine on both counts.

Will it change my personality?

I think the thing I was most worried about before I went on medication was that I'd be somehow numbed to the world. I wouldn't be able to write or I wouldn't feel things as deeply. This is a common concern. Whenever I talk to friends who are contemplating going to see their doctor about medication, it is one of their primary fears. But for all the various issues I've had with my medication, this has never been one of them.

Medication is not designed to numb you against the world or make you feel less. It's intended to rid you of depression or anxiety or mania, to make you better able to cope. In fact, it doesn't make you *feel* anything in particular; it just makes you more stable. It evens you out; if anything, it makes it easier for you to actually be yourself again.

What happens if it doesn't work?

Don't panic. Medication often takes a while to kick in, and it may be a month or two before you see a real differ-ence. A partner of mine told me that it had once taken eighteen months before his medication settled down and started to make him feel better. That's not to say you should wait this long if you think your meds aren't helping, but it's worth bearing in mind if you're feeling worried or impatient.

Plus, the first medication you try may not be for you, and that's fine. Try again: go back to your doctor; tell them it's not working out and try something else. If the pattern keeps repeating, rethink your options together with your doctor, who may be able to further develop your treatment plan.

What will happen when/if I come off them?

It's always best to come off your medication with the help or guidance of a doctor or therapist. I have learned from bitter, bitter experience that this is far preferable to going cold turkey. Cold turkey sucks. Cold turkey makes you feel physically and mentally terrible. Cold turkey is the worst.

If you do want to do it alone, make sure you don't just suddenly stop taking your medication one day. Start by taking half doses or taking it every other day until you slowly stop. I don't recommend doing this without speaking to a doctor first, though. You're absolutely entitled to make up your own mind about this; even if they disagree, if you feel it's right for you to go meds-free, then you do that thing. But the physical side effects of coming off medication can be just as severe or uncomfortable as the mental side effects, so be careful.

* * *

Medication can be seen as a panacea, a complete antidote to whatever ailment you have. Documentaries and books about mental health stress that you *need* to be on medication; it's one of the first suggestions many doctors make, regardless of any underlying pressures or stresses you're experiencing at the time. To an extent, this is good – treating mental illness just as you would a physical one can be demystifying, destigmatising. You'd take antibiotics if you had an infection or a virus, so why not treat mental health problems in exactly the same way?

But sometimes medication doesn't work; and sometimes it doesn't suit your lifestyle. Or maybe you just don't want to be on it. These are all fine and legitimate. There's no need to feel pressured into doing what other people see as the 'right thing' for you. If you're making a responsible, informed and considered choice about medication, then it's your prerogative.

If you've never tried medication, however, I think my advice would probably be to give it a go. The reasons why people are resistant are absolutely understandable – I've been medication-free for several periods of my life (including now). But there is always the chance – quite a strong chance too – that medication *will* help. If it doesn't, it doesn't; that's a bummer, but it might happen. And in that case you're well within your rights to not want to be on anything, and to take charge of your mental health in a different way. But it's always worth finding that out for yourself first.

Therapy

As a complete narcissist, you would have thought I'd enjoy therapy. After all, the point of it is that you sit and talk about yourself for an hour, while a neutral party listens and asks questions about how you feel and what you think. It's the closest thing most of us are gonna get to being interviewed by Oprah, essentially. Yet, somehow, it's not quite as fun or glamorous as that.

Therapy forces me to examine how and why I do things. There's no self-deception involved here, just cold, hard truths. Yes, your therapist is (or at least should be) neutral, but that doesn't mean they can't ask you incredibly awkward and searching questions. Less Oprah, more police interrogation.

I'm not being entirely serious, but these things do somewhat underlie why I have trouble going to therapy – because it genuinely *asks* something of me. Taking medication is a pretty value-free transaction – you put the pill in your mouth, you swallow, your mood is hopefully altered for the better. Therapy is harder. Therapy requires you to question your motives and work to adjust the imbalances in your behaviour and your thoughts. Therapy requires you to be honest with yourself. And therapy requires you to take the time and effort to genuinely improve yourself as a person.

I *want* to go to therapy because every time I've done so for a prolonged period of time it's really helped me. I *want* to be brave enough to look at my life and my choices and ask myself questions that need asking. And sometimes I am. Other times? I am not. If medication is a stiff drink after a bad day, therapy is a long, hard look at yourself in the mirror the morning after.

What you need to know about therapy

- **There are lots of choices**

There is an unimaginably huge number of choices of therapy and therapists. You may imagine yourself reclining on a couch while a Freudian psychoanalyst asks you about your childhood, and this may seem completely unappealing, but the range of options extends way beyond that.

There's CBT (Cognitive Behavioural Therapy), which seeks to change the way you think and behave through the examination of thoughts, feelings and behaviour. There's psychoanalysis, which most closely resembles the Freudian stereotype. There's talk therapy, where, rather predictably, you sit and talk through your issues. There are specific therapies for sexual dysfunction, anxiety, anger management and more. There's hypnotherapy and art therapy, dialectic behavioural therapy. Essentially, there are a million types of therapies and therapists for a variety of different issues.

So, do your research. What do you want to achieve during therapy? Do you want to resolve issues from your past or do you want to focus on developing coping mechanisms for the future? What kind of therapist would make you feel most comfortable? Do you want a male or female therapist? Do you have any particular requirements that might be worth considering? Do you want a therapist specifically trained to deal with LGBT issues, for example, or someone who's specialised in treating people who have experienced sexual assault or abuse? These may not seem like things that might affect your therapeutic journey too much, but they really can; having someone you're completely comfortable with is the whole point, so you may as well be as specific as you can.

The British Association of Counselling and Psychotherapy's online 'Find a Therapist' function, which you can find on their website, can be useful here. It filters therapists not only by area, but also by the reasons for seeking therapy (options include sexual dysfunction, PTSD, self-harm and many more), type of approach (CBT, behavioural, psycho-dynamic, etc.) and type of client (families, couples, young people). This allows you to approach therapy in either an extremely focused way or, if you're not sure what you're looking for yet, in a broader sense. If you're still not sure, email or call a few different therapists to see whether or not they're the right fit for you.

Making the effort to find a therapist I can relate to on a personal, psychological and intellectual level has made all the difference for me; as with any ongoing relationship, it's important that you do genuinely relate to one another. Being liked isn't the point, obviously, but having an affable relationship with my therapist is actually very empowering. We're not *friends* because that's not the point of the rela-tionship, but I can say that I feel liked, respected and, most of all, *listened to*. It means I actually look forward to sessions I previously would have dreaded; and I feel validated when I speak to him. (He also laughs at my bad jokes, which I suspect he does out of politeness rather than genuine amusement, but it helps.)

- **You will have to work hard**

Somewhat annoyingly, therapy is hard work. You'll be forced to consider what you think and why, and sometimes you'll have to examine your behaviour. This is sometimes revelatory, but often painful, and sometimes embarrassing or shameful.

You may also have to work through particularly difficult things. You may have experienced sexual assault for example, and feel it's worth exploring with a therapist. You may have been putting off dealing with certain emotions or situations because it was the best way for you to cope at the time. This is fine, but therapy is often predicated on tackling these issues. It can be tough.

A good and responsible therapist will be sensitive to all of this, and will understand how hard – and sometimes awkward – it will be for you to deal with and talk about these issues. That may not make it much easier for you to speak about your problems, but it can be reassuring to keep in mind when you're struggling to voice your feelings.

- **There are no easy answers, and there's certainly no cure**

If you were expecting a transactional exchange – input hard, emotional work, receive emotional revelation – you may be disappointed. While you may feel better for having therapy (and I certainly have), it won't be instantaneous and it will never make you not mentally ill. Some issues can be resolved, but others simply can't.

What therapy *can* do, though, is make you feel more stable and provide you with a steadier ground on which to build a more settled life. It can give you coping mechanisms that can actively prevent – or at least minimise – future episodes. I will always have bipolar, but I won't always seek comfort or distraction in the damaging ways I've relied on in the past because therapy is teaching me how to at least attempt to deal with them in a healthier way. I've had moments of genuine, awe-inspiring revelation – eureka moments that have felt at first transcendentally important and then maddeningly obvious. Often, after these moments, I find myself asking myself why the fuck I wasn't able previously to work out what was now such a clear and self-evident truth. The answer is because nobody had asked me the right question, and I hadn't known how to direct myself towards it.

I have had numerous bad experiences with therapy, which may seem off-putting, but, as I've said, perseverance has really been key for me. Though I've had what feel like endless boring and sometimes potentially damaging sessions, I'm now back in therapy and finding it – shock horror – genuinely useful.

My current therapist combines CBT-type techniques with psychodynamic and humanistic approaches, which is working really well for me. He asks me probing, interesting questions, he respects my boundaries, he constantly checks that I feel safe and able to carry on with sessions, especially when we're discussing difficult issues. Since I've started seeing him I've consistently felt better equipped to deal with my problems, and have been far more self-critical in a way that's been very constructive and productive. I feel like I'm constantly being encouraged to challenge my motivations and behaviours within the confines of an extremely safe space. I feel as if I can actually take responsibility for my mental health. I feel – for once – more stable.

Relapsing

Relapsing is one of my worst fears. Give me shark-infested waters or make me walk a tightrope across the Grand Canyon any day; make me stand with no pants on in front of a room full of people I went to school with . . . Just please, god, don't let me relapse.

For those who don't know, relapsing essentially means moving away from a period of stability and contentedness to a period of ill mental health. This can happen at any point – you may have been feeling better again for a week or a year, and you can still experience a relapse.

A guide to relapsing

Relapsing (which has happened to me often) is the number-one reason why I resolutely refuse to subscribe to the 'it-gets-better' school of thought when it comes to mental illness. The thinking *behind* it is great – namely, the idea that you won't feel like this for ever. And that's true; you won't. You will feel better than you do at your very worst. But that doesn't mean you'll be better for ever, or that you won't feel that way again.

That said, there are plenty of things that can help or mitigate a relapse.

- **Watch out for triggers**

  Before you even begin to experience a relapse, it's important to identify potential triggers. For me, break-ups often lead to terrible depressive episodes, and warm weather to mania. Going out a lot, and thus losing sleep, can also make me manic, as can overexercising. Drinking too much can make me depressed – just one particularly maudlin hangover can transport me from healthy and stable to fucked-up mess in no time at all. And the list goes on.

It's taken me quite a long time to recognise all of these triggers, and they're only the tip of the iceberg; there are many, many seemingly innocuous things that can set off an episode for me. Be mindful of yours; if you can, try to avoid them as much as possible.

It's also important to note, however, that a relapse is often not prompted by anything. Sometimes absolutely nothing you've done causes you to feel bad again – it just happens. But it is useful to know what you need to keep an eye on.

• Have a plan

I've mentioned this before, but I can't stress it enough.

It's best to make both wellness and emergency plans with a professional, preferably your therapist. This can include a list of emergency contacts, a process for contacting people if you start feeling bad again or a list of self-care ideas.

Make a list or a spreadsheet or fill a notebook full of pretty doodles and scrapbooked pictures; whatever works for you. Keep it somewhere safe, so you'll know exactly what to do when you need help. Share this with somebody else who you trust. You essentially need to create an encyclopaedia for yourself and your mental health.

• Get help as soon as possible

If you feel that you are at the beginning of a relapse *get help as soon as you can*. Like me, you may be prone to writing bad moods off as nothing more than a bad day, but it is vital that you keep an eye on yourself and your moods in order to spot wider patterns. One bad day is normal; a week or two weeks or a month of bad days is not. Struggling to get out of bed one morning or dreading work once a week is fine; feeling like that every single day is not.

Once you start to see these patterns emerging, go and speak to someone. Mention it to a friend or to your therapist. Stopping depression or mania in their earliest stages isn't easy, but it's not impossible. And it is much, much less difficult than trying to squirm your way out of a particularly bad episode.

• Treat yourself kindly

Please, please remember: this is not the end of the world. It can be so disheartening when you've worked hard at recovery and you feel like you're back at square one. It's heartbreaking, actually – like you did all that work for nothing, that you're going to feel this way forever and that you're absolutely unfixable. But none of these things is true.

The fact that you feel bad now doesn't undo all of the good you've done. If you've worked hard at recovery, then you'll know more about your mental illness than you can possibly imagine: you understand your moods better, you've gone to therapy, you've worked through issues, you've managed to maintain a stable and happy life for however long. And none of this is just suddenly invalidated because you're having a bad episode. It's taught you things that you might not be able to put into practice immediately, but that will help you get better more quickly and efficiently. You know about SMART goals, so you can put them into action; and you know about self-care. So, although it might feel like you're at square one again, you're not. You've skipped back a few spaces, sure, but you're nowhere near the beginning.

* * *

My fear of relapsing may seem irrational to outsiders. Considering I've been ill for so long – *so* long – and have come out the other side of every major breakdown relatively unscathed, it should have lost some of its ability to terrify me by now. It hasn't.

Every moment of happiness is overshadowed by the threat of relapse; every time I plan for my future I have to factor in the spectre of a dreaded breakdown. When I think about where I want to be in ten years, of course I wonder and worry about my career and my relationships, whether I'll ever earn enough to buy a house or if I'll eventually pass my driving test. But in among all of that stuff – the regular twenty-something stuff – I think, What happens to my career if I have to take time off to recover from a suicide attempt? Will my relationships survive if I have a particularly bad manic episode? Will I even be alive, more to the point? Will I be able to keep surviving episode after episode of bad mental health?

My multiple trips to psychiatric hospitals and doctors' surgeries and the horrible, drug-addled lows of my life should probably have served as lessons. Y'know – things can only get better! When you hit rock bottom, the only way is up! That kind of thing. All of these things should serve as vaccinations against fear; I should be immune. I know what to do, after all; I know the score.

But when you've 'recovered', when you've slowly rebuilt your life again, the idea that it could all disappear is even more terrifying. I have a pretty nice life now; I have a flat I like living in. I get to write about things that I care about, and people actually pay me money for it. I'm nervous to say it, but I genuinely love my life. What if it's all taken away again?

But you know what? That's not how I should look at it. My flat and my career, this book and my friends, are not things that *can* be taken away from me. In a literal sense, obviously, I could lose my job or fall out with my friends. Every copy of this book could be destroyed in a simultaneous pulp-plant/hard-drive deletion accident. But in a metaphorical sense – because yes, we're getting deep here – they're immovable.

What all of these things represent is a talent that I have, and that everyone who's mentally ill has, for rebuilding. It might not be a talent that we want – I'd rather *not* know how rock bottom feels, or how exactly to proceed from that point. But we have it out of necessity. Everything we have – however much or little – is testament to our continued existence, and the strength that that necessitates.

Sometimes recovery feels impossible, and once you're there it feels tentative and unsteady and altogether ready to completely collapse. We all know that it's a distinct possibility – that unless you're one of the incredibly lucky people who experience only one period of bad mental health in their lives, you're likely to feel like shit again at some point. But if and when you do, go forward with the knowledge that you *can* rebuild things, you *can* cope. You know how to look after yourself when you're feeling like shit. You know what to tell a doctor. You know how to tell your mum or your partner or your teachers how you feel and what help you need. You understand yourself better as a result of what you've been through; you may even have learned things about yourself that you'd previously underestimated. Being mentally ill isn't fun or enjoyable by any stretch of the imagination, but it can give you a deeper wellspring of understanding, a way of navigating the world slightly differently. After a while, you'll know how better to help yourself and you'll be able to do it more efficiently, more eloquently, more sensitively. You might even like yourself (or at least a bit more).

In other words? You got this.

RESOURCES

Websites and Phone Lines

Samaritans: http://www.samaritans.org/; call 116 123; email jo@samaritans.org

Mind: http://www.mind.org.uk; call 0300 123 3393; text 86463

Rethink: https://www.rethink.org; call 0300 5000 927

CALM: https://www.thecalmzone.net; call 0800 58 58 58 nationwide or 0808 802 58 58 in London

The Mix: http://www.themix.org.uk/; call 0808 808 4994

The Mental Health Foundation: http://www.mentalhealth.org.uk/

Time to Change: http://www.time-to-change.org.uk

Selfharm UK: http://www.selfharm.co.uk

LifeSIGNS: www.lifesigns.org.uk

The British Association for Counselling and Psychotherapy: http://www.bacp.co.uk

Mood Diaries

As I wrote, mood diaries can be really useful both for you and your clinician or therapist. There are online resources that help you to keep a mood diary, as well as several apps, or you can create one using a Google Docs spreadsheet. You can also keep an old-fashioned mood diary on paper; below is an example:

Day, time and location	Mood/Emotion	Comments (Who were you with? What were you doing? What went through your mind?)
Wednesday, 11am, at school	*Unhappy - 3/10*	*Told off at school. Felt humiliated in front of classmates*
Thursday, 9pm, at home	*Lonely - 4/10*	*On my own, spending time on the Internet, wished I was seeing friends*

Breathing and Relaxation Exercises

There are so many different breathing exercises you can try, but here are just a few examples that have helped me in the past.

The basics

* Lie or sit somewhere comfortable. If you're sitting, cross your legs and keep your back straight and shoulders back. Close your eyes.

* Breathe in deeply through your nose, feeling the breath flow from as far down your body as you can. Breathe in for five seconds, or to the count of five (as long as this is comfortable for you).

* Hold your breath for two seconds.

* Breathe out through your mouth, again counting to five.

* Do this for several minutes, or for as long as you need to feel calmer.

Belly breathing

* Lying down, place one hand on your stomach and one on your chest.

* Gently breathe out, letting your upper body relax as you do it.

* Pause for a few seconds.

- Inhale through your nose for a few seconds and pause again. Repeat, focusing on relaxing your muscles.

Progressive muscle relaxation

This is the exercise I find most helpful. It completely calms me down and I often use it to help me go to sleep. You can do this sitting in a chair or lying down, although if you lie down, you may also fall asleep.

The first step is actually making your body *more* tense:

- Methodically work your way up your body, from your feet, tensing your muscles as you go.

- Squeeze your feet up as hard as you can . . . and relax.

- Squeeze your leg muscles as hard as you can . . . and relax.

- Move all the way up your body, tensing and relaxing every part for five or ten seconds.

SMART Goal Table

SPECIFIC – what is the goal? Break it down into several small steps
MEASURABLE – how are you going to measure it? Are you aiming to cut down on something or quit completely? Put a figure on it.
ACHIEVABLE – write down the steps you need to take to make this happen.
RELEVANT – what resources do you need to achieve this? How are you going to do it? Write this down.
TIMELY – when do you want to do it by? 1pm? Tomorrow morning? The end of the year?

ACKNOWLEDGEMENTS

First off I have to thank my wonderful, patient, tenacious, brilliant agent Robyn Drury, who was not only the catalyst for me writing this book but has also dealt with numerous mini-breakdowns and thousands of emails over the last eighteen months with patience and good humour, and never once replied to a stupid question of mine with 'can't you just Google it?!' as she probably could and should have done. I'd also like to thank everyone else at Diane Banks for being so supportive throughout the whole process, despite the fact I had absolutely no idea what I was doing at any given moment.

I'd also like to thank the entire team at Hodder & Stoughton generally and Yellow Kite specifically – Liz Gough, Becca Mundy and especially my editor Maddy Price, who instantly understood what I wanted to do and say, and somehow, magically, coaxed a vaguely decent book out of me. Thank you all for making the stressful experience of writing a book actually really fun.

To everyone who agreed to be interviewed for the book: Felicity de Vere for her medical know-how, Billy MacFarlane for talking to me about teaching, Jonny Gabriel for talking to me about his brother, Simon, and everyone else who anonymously shared anecdotes, stories and experiences with me while I wrote the book.

I also want to say thank you to all of my friends, who have put up with me saying variants upon 'I am writing a book and I am stressed about writing the book' for nearly two straight years. (Sorry about that.)

Firstly, everyone (and there are way too many to mention by name) from the creepy dog crew/alt Twitter, for distracting me all day and inviting me to brunch every weekend when I should definitely have been writing this book. All my Berlin friends, who had to listen to me talk about nothing but edits for about six weeks. For proofreading, suggestions, thought-provoking debates, general encouragement and pep talks I'd also like to say thanks to George Berridge, Tristan Cross, Josh Hall, Merlin Jobst, Sarah-Louise Kelly, Tom Mendelsohn, Alison Terpstra, Jack Urwin and James Vincent. This is the only time I'm ever going to be sincere to any of you (and in actual print, ugh) but I love you all and am deeply appreciative of all the help and support you've given me re: the book and also re: my being crazy. Special thanks to George Allen and Tilly Steele, the two people I could never live without, two brilliant, sparkling, fascinating and talented people who have made me a way better person simply by allowing me to be myself.

To my therapist, Anthony Rhone, who somehow managed to help me start to craft a vaguely human-like form out of what was previously a weird, amorphous, dysfunctional blob.

To all of my family I want to say thanks but also sorry – thank you for putting up with me, looking after me and bailing me out of every stupid mess I've ever made; sorry that you had to.

ACKNOWLEDGEMENTS

Most of all I'd like to thank anybody who has ever got in touch with me to talk about mental health: people's sisters and wives and boyfriends and best friends who wanted to know how to help, people who wanted to tell me their stories or ask me for advice or just talk to someone else who gets it, people who are desperately ill and people who are in recovery. This book is about you and for you, and I hope that by telling my story I've done justice to yours.

INDEX

addictions 2, 121–22, 123, 124

air, fresh 41, 170, 171

alcohol and alcohol misuse
  author's personal journey 13, 31–32, 102–3, 106
  cutting down 52–53, 59–60
  impact on mental health 107–8, 122
  public attitudes towards 121–22, 126
  saying "no" 107–8
  as self-harm 132

anticonvulsants 197

antidepressants 194, 196, 197, 198

antipsychotics 195, 197, 198

anxiety
  coping strategies 45, 48
  dehydration resembling 43
  exam 117, 119
  medication 197

promotion factors 53, 64, 107, 181

public attitudes towards 134

aripiprazole 199

aromatherapy 45–46, 129

author's personal journey
  alcohol misuse 13, 31–32, 102–3, 106
  dating mistakes 65–68
  depression 2, 3–6, 16, 30–33, 35–36, 90–95, 111
  diagnosis 1–2, 5, 9, 16, 17, 21
  dysfunctionality 35
  early symptoms 2–3
  exams 115
  family history of mental illness 152–54, 154–55
  family's handling of mental illness 149–152, 154, 160–61, 162–63
  flatmate's callousness 105–6
  friendships 164–66

GP's lack of understanding 4
  Internet use 104, 169,
    176–79, 183, 189
  manic episodes 5–6, 18–19,
    104–5
  medication 194–96, 197–98
  mental illness as excuse
    17–18, 19–20
  'outsider' label, generating
    14–15
  performative 'madness'
    16–17
  post break-up behaviour
    13–14
  psychotic episodes 12–13,
    30, 104–5
  recovery 191–92, 192–93
  relapse, fear of 207, 210–11
  relationship challenges 83,
    84–87
  schooldays 2–3, 14–15, 89,
    90–95
  self-harm reduction 127,
    132–33
  self-harming 2, 14, 91, 94,
    95, 104–6, 122, 123,
    124–25
  self-image–mental illness ties
    10–11, 15–16
  suicide attempts/thoughts 4,
    14, 135–37, 147
  therapy 201–2, 204, 206
  tidying up 45
  uncleanliness 17–18, 31,

    32–33, 34–35, 36–37,
    111–12
  university 88–89, 99–107,
    110–12, 120
autonomy 78, 158, 161–62

bathing 41–42
being your real self 100, 110,
    167–68
bipolar disorder 1, 28–29, 134,
    153, 193, 197
BoJack Horseman 83–84
breathing exercises 48, 119,
    129, 216–17
British Association for
    Counselling and
    Psychotherapy 76, 213

caffeine 52–53, 55
CALM 213
care packages 174–75
carers
  autonomy vs. best interests
    161–63
  challenges 159–163
  emergency plans 78
  expecting hard times 76–77
  helping suicidal person
    145–47
  listening 78–79, 175
  not taking things personally
    77
  patience 161
  practical help 170–75

research 77–78
things not to say 79–83
see also family; friends
citalopram 194, 198
confidentiality 97
contraception 74–75

dating
    author's personal journey
        65–68
    being your real self 86–87
    feeling unlovable 82–83
    mentally ill partners 76–82
    paranoia 84, 85–86
    sex 71–76
    telling about your illness
        64–71
dehydration 43
depression
    anthropomorphising 92–93
    author's personal journey 2,
        3–6, 16, 30–33, 35–36,
        90–95, 111
    characteristics 92
    defining 35–36, 91
    libido, effect on 72–73
    prevalence 90
    stigmatisation 134
    understandings of 35–36
    vs. despair 136
despair 38, 136
diagnosis
    author's personal journey
        1–2, 5, 9, 16, 17, 21

benefits 27–29
    as first step to help 27
    limitations 12
    obtaining 21–27
    self-understanding 28–29
    sharing with friends/family
        28
    sliding scale 192
    vs. self-identity 26
diaries 23, 50–51, 52, 55–56,
    184–85, 214–15
dressing 42–43
drugs (illegal) 102, 121–22, 126,
    132
drugs (prescription) *see* medica-
    tion
DSM (Diagnostic and Statistical
    Manual of Mental
    Disorders) 10
dysfunctionality 32–35, 36–37

eating 46, 52–53, 173–74
emergency plans 51–52, 78,
    139, 208
empathy 105
exams 98–99, 114–120
excuse, mental illness as 17–18,
    19–20
exercise 47, 53–55, 129

face washing 42
family
    history of mental illness
        152–55

how to live together 155–59
impact of mental illness on
    148–152, 154–55, 160–61
involving 97
keeping in touch 109–10
see also carers
finances 114
Find a Therapist website 76,
    204
fluoxetine 194
food 46, 52–53, 173–74
fresh air 41, 170, 171
friends
    author's personal journey
        164–66
    being honest with 167–68
    challenges in making/keeping
        163–64
    going out with 169–170
    importance 167
    keeping in touch 109–10
    online 168–69, 176, 178
    sharing your diagnosis with
        28
    support groups 57
friends, supporting mentally ill
    145–47, 170–75; *see also*
    carers

gifts 42–43, 174
goal-setting 57–60, 112–13, 133,
    218
going outside 41, 169–170,
    170–71

GP appointment
    being persistent 25–27
    booking and attending
        22–23
    preparing for 23–25
GPs
    bringing questions to
        188–89
    finding the right one 27
    good and bad 4, 22, 24
    mental health training
        26–27

help, asking for
    with exams 117–18
    from friends/family 78
    from a GP 22–27
    offline 188–89
    after a relapse 209
    from a schoolteacher 95–99
    see also talking to others
helplines 213
honesty 70, 167–68, 202
house rules 159
hydration 43
hypersexuality 74–76

identity 10–11, 15–16, 67
'in-case-of-emergency' lists
    51–52, 78, 139, 208
Internet
    author's personal journey
        104, 169, 176–79, 183,
        189

doing research 77–78, 185, 187–89, 198
finding a therapist 204
as hindrance 180–81
information checking 1 87–89
monitoring use 184–85, 189–190
not replacement for therapist/ doctor 185
online friendships 168–69, 179
privacy settings 182–83
resources for suicidal people 138
safety 181–86
self-care information 39
time off 185–86
website blockers 182
websites, useful 213
see also social media
introspection 62, 129–130

kindness to yourself 48–49, 119, 209

lack of understanding
about suicide 140–45
in friends/colleagues 105, 164
in healthcare professionals 4, 24, 25–26
in partners 79–82
libido 71–76

Life SIGNS 213
listening 5, 78–79, 146, 175, 204
lithium 197

manic episodes 5–6, 18–19, 20, 37, 104–5, 160
medication
author's personal journey 194–96, 197–98
coming off 200
deciding for or against 201
effect on personality 199
hiding when suicidal 138–39
not working 199–200
side-effects 198–99
time for effectiveness 199–200
types 197
use only doctor-prescribed 197–98
mental health education/aware- ness 140
Mental Health Foundation 213
Mind 213
misdiagnoses 1–2
The Mix 188, 213
mood diaries 50–51, 52, 184, 214–15
Morrissey 15, 83, 178
myths about suicide 140–41
'attention seeking' 143
'suicide is selfish' 141–42
'talkers vs. doers' 142
'weakness' 143–45

'outsider,' being an 14–15
overidentification 11, 70–71

panic attacks 45–46, 48, 179
parents *see* family
paroxetine 194
partners, information for
     sex 71–74
     things not to say 79–82
     things to do 76–79
personal hygiene 41–42
phone lines, helpful 213
PHQ-9 Depression Test 24
Plath, Sylvia 15, 122
psychiatrists 5, 21, 26, 189
psychotic episodes 12–13, 21,
     30, 104–5
pyjamas 42–43

quetiapine 195–96

rebuilding 211–12
recovery
     author's personal journey
          191–92, 192–93
     medication 197–201
     rebuilding 211–12
     sliding scale 9–10, 192, 1
          93
     therapy 202–6
relapse
     defining 207
     fear of 207, 210–11
     getting help 209

planning for 208
     self-compassion 209–10
     triggers 207–8
relationships, romantic/sexual *see*
     dating
relaxation techniques 119,
     217
research 50, 77–78, 185,
     187–89, 198
Rethink 213
rubbish collection 45
rumination 153

safety 75, 130–32, 138–39,
     181–86
Samaritans 138, 213
school
     asking a teacher for help
          95–99
     author's personal journey
          2–3, 14–15, 89, 90–95
     help with schoolwork and
          exams 98–99
     mental health education/
          awareness 140
     prevalence of pupil mental
          illness 90
self-care tips, advanced 49–50
     'in-case-of-emergency' list
          51–52
     doing research 50
     eating 52–53
     exercising 53–55
     goal-setting 57–60

mood diary 50–51
sleeping 55–56
support groups 57
therapy 56–57
self-care tips, basic
    aromatherapy 45–46
    bathing/showering 41–42
    breathing exercises 48
    defining "self-care" 38–40
    to-do lists 44
    dressing 42–43
    drinking water 43
    eating 46
    face washing 42
    fresh air 41
    movement/exercise 47
    rubbish collection 45
    self-congratulation 49
    stretching 43
    sunlight 40–41
    talking to others 47–48
    tidying up 44–45
self-compassion 48–49, 119,
    209
self-congratulation 49
self-harming
    as addiction 2, 124
    author's personal journey 2,
        14, 91, 94, 95, 104–6, 122,
        123, 124–25
    condescending attitudes
        towards 65, 124, 125–26
    coping strategies 127–130
    gender stereotyped 124

impact on relationships 86
motives 122, 125
prevalence 125
reaction of horror towards
    126–27
safety and first aid 130–32
teachers' legal duties 97
theories 123
self-image 10–11, 15–16, 67
self-understanding 28–29, 50,
    212
self-worth 87, 211–12
Selfharm UK 213
sertraline 194
sex 71–76
showering 41–42
sleep-hygiene 55–56
SMART goals 58–60, 133,
    218
Smiths 15, 88
social activities 169–170
social media
    author's personal journey 18,
        103, 104, 178–180
    privacy settings 183–84
    staying in touch 110
    taking breaks from 186
    talking to others 47, 48,
        168–69
    see also Internet
space, your own 157–58
SSRIs (Selective Serotonin
    Reuptake Inhibitors) 194,
    197

stretching 43
Styron, William 36
suicide/suicidal thoughts
    arguments against 133–34
    author's personal journey 4,
        14, 135–37, 147
    impact on relationships 86
    myths 140–45
    stigmatisation 133, 134,
        141–42
    strategies to get through
        138–39
    supporting a friend through
        145–47
    teachers' legal duties 97
sunlight 40–41
support groups 57

talking to others
    friends/family 109–10, 130,
        152, 158–59, 168–69, 179,
        180
    GPs 23–25
    as self-care strategy 47–48
    support groups 57
    teachers 95–99
    therapists 56–57, 201–6
    when you are suicidal 138
    see also asking for help
teachers 95–99
ten-minutes-by-ten-minutes
    technique 128, 133
therapy
    attending 56–57

author's personal journey
    201–2, 204, 206
    benefits 205–6
    limitations 205
    personal challenges 202, 205
    therapist 204
    types 203–4
tidying up 41, 44–45, 112–13,
    171–72
Time to Change 213
to-do lists 44, 56

uncleanliness 17–18, 32–37,
    111–12
university
    alcohol 107–8
    author's personal journey
        88–89, 99–107, 110–12,
        120
    finances 114
    living alone 110–12
    practical solutions 113
    preparation 112
    prevalence of student mental
        illness 89
    staying in touch with friends/
        family 109–10
    stocking up on essentials
        113–14
    tidying up 112–13
    unique experience 110

water 43, 53
websites, useful 76, 213